The **Solar System**
and the **Stars**

WORLD ALMANAC® LIBRARY

Please visit our website at: **www.worldalmanaclibrary.com**
For a free color catalog describing World Almanac® Library's list of high-quality books and multimedia programs, call 1-800-848-2928 (USA) or 1-800-461-9120 (Canada). World Almanac® Library's Fax: (414) 332-3567.

The editors at World Almanac® Library would like to thank Greg Walz-Chojnacki, a writer, editor, and consultant in the study of astronomy and space technology, for the technical expertise and advice he brought to the production of this book.

Library of Congress Cataloging-in-Publication Data

The solar system and the stars. — North American ed.
    p. cm. — (21st century science)
    Includes bibliographical references and index.
    ISBN 0-8368-5004-1 (lib. bdg.)
    1. Solar system—Juvenile literature. [1. Solar system. 2. Planets.] I. Title. II. Series.
    QB501.3.S655   2001
    523.2—dc21   2001031441

This North American edition first published in 2001 by
World Almanac® Library
330 West Olive Street, Suite 100
Milwaukee, WI 53212 USA

Created and produced as the *Visual Guide to the Wonders of Our Universe* by
QA INTERNATIONAL

329 rue de la Commune Ouest, 3ᵉ étage
Montreal, Québec
Canada H2Y 2E1
Tel: (514) 499-3000 Fax: (514) 499-3010
www.qa-international.com

© QA International, 2001

Editorial Director: François Fortin
Executive Editor: Serge D'Amico
Art Director: Marc Lalumière
Graphic Designer: Anne Tremblay
Writers: Nathalie Fredette, Claude Lafleur
Computer Graphic Artists: Mamadou Togola, Alain Lemire, Hoang-Khanh Le,
Ara Yazedjian, Mélanie Boivin, Jean-Yves Ahern, Michel Rouleau
Page Layout: Lucie Mc Brearty, Véronique Boisvert,
Geneviève Théroux Béliveau
Researchers: Anne-Marie Villeneuve, Anne-Marie Brault
Astronomy Reviewer: Louie Bernstein
Copy Editor: Jane Broderick
Production: Gaétan Forcillo, Guylaine Houle
Prepress: Tony O'Riley
Translation: Kathe Roth
World Almanac® Library Editor: David K. Wright
World Almanac® Library Art Direction: Karen Knutson
Cover Design: Katherine A. Kroll

Photo credits: abbreviations: t = top, c = center, b = bottom, r = right, l = left.
pp. 11 (tl), 30 (br): JSC/NASA; pp. 17 (b), 39 (tr), 41 (Mimas, Dione, Iapetus, & Rhea):
NSSDC/NASA; pp. 18 (c & br), 34 (cr & br), 35 (cr), 40 (Ganymede, Callisto, & bl), 41
(Titan), 42 (Umbriel, Ariel, Oberon, Titania, & tl), 43 (tr & cr), 44 (bl): JPL/NASA; p. 31 (bl):
KSC/NASA; p. 34 (cl, cc, & bl): U.S. Geological Survey/NASA; p. 35 (bl & bc): IVV/NASA;
p. 37 (tr): D. Roddy/Lunar and Planetary Institute/IVV/NASA; p. 37 (cl): Laboratory
photograph/Courtesy of Russell W. Kempton/New England Meteoritical Services, Robert Haag
Meteorite Collection/FOTOSMITH; p. 37 (cr): Agence spatiale canadienne: comité consultatif
sur les météorites et les impacts; p. 37 (bl): Robert Haag Meteorite Collection/FOTOSMITH;
pp. 39 (BR), 51 (tr): HST/NASA; p. 40 (Io & Europa): NASA; pp. 42 (Miranda), 43 (b): U.S.
Geological Survey/NASA/JPL/NASA; pp. 47 (tr), 61 (br): Association of Universities for
Research in Astronomy Inc. (AURA), all rights reserved; p. 51 (tl): H. Bond (STScI)/NASA;
p. 51 (bl): T. Nakajima (CalTech)/S. Durrance (Johns Hopkins University)/NASA; pp. 53 (tr),
57 (t): © Anglo-Australian Observatory; p. 53 (bl): Max-Planck Institute for Extraterrestrial
Physics; p. 55 (br): L. Ferrarese (Johns Hopkins University)/NASA; p. 56 (tc): Mount Wilson
observatory/NASA; p. 56 (bl): J. Hester and P. Scowen (Arizona State University)/NASA;
p. 60 (cl): Dominique Dierick and Dick De la Marche/NASA

Printed in Canada

1 2 3 4 5 6 7 8 9 05 04 03 02 01

Table of Contents

Although it seems incredibly big from our point of view, the Solar System is infinitely small on the scale of the Universe. Nevertheless, studying it is invaluable for acquiring knowledge of the cosmos as a whole. After all, our Sun, the fiery ball around which the planets orbit, is a star just like any of the "astronomical" number of stars in the Universe!

The Solar System

The Solar System

Our little corner of the Universe

The Solar System includes one star (the Sun), nine planets, about sixty natural satellites orbiting the planets, thousands of asteroids (small rocky objects), millions of comets (lumps of dust and frozen gas), billions of meteoroids, and interplanetary dust and gas.

THE MILKY WAY

Our Solar System is on the edge of the Milky Way, our galaxy. The Milky Way stretches some 7.5 billion billion miles (12 billion billion kilometers), or 7.5 million million million miles (12 million million million km). If we think of the Milky Way as a beach, our Solar System is but a grain of sand.

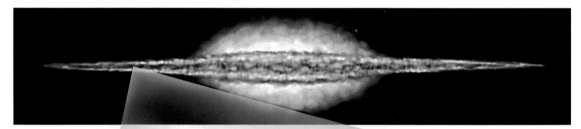

THE OUTER PLANETS

The giant planets farthest away from the Sun are gaseous globes (made mainly of hydrogen and helium) that all have rings and a number of satellites.

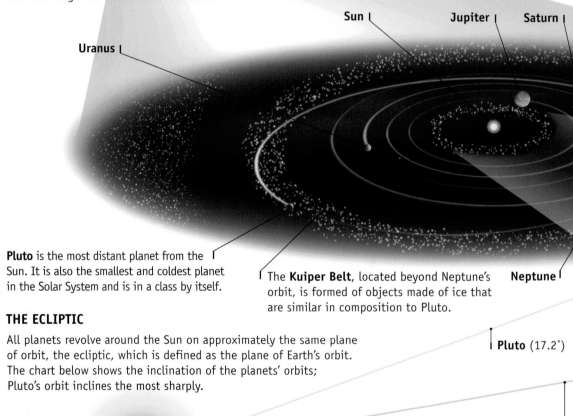

Uranus | Sun | Jupiter | Saturn |

Pluto is the most distant planet from the Sun. It is also the smallest and coldest planet in the Solar System and is in a class by itself.

The **Kuiper Belt**, located beyond Neptune's orbit, is formed of objects made of ice that are similar in composition to Pluto.   Neptune |

THE ECLIPTIC

All planets revolve around the Sun on approximately the same plane of orbit, the ecliptic, which is defined as the plane of Earth's orbit. The chart below shows the inclination of the planets' orbits; Pluto's orbit inclines the most sharply.

Pluto (17.2°)

solar equator

Earth (0°) | Jupiter (1.3°) | Mars (1.9°) | Venus (3.4°) |
Uranus (0.8°) | Neptune (1.8°) | Saturn (2.5°) | Mercury (7°) |

CELESTIAL OBJECTS

In general, a star (such as the Sun) is a heavenly body that emits a great quantity of energy (light and heat). A planet ❶ is a body that orbits a star and reflects part of that energy; a natural satellite ❷ (or moon) revolves around a planet. All nine planets orbit around the Sun in a counter-clockwise direction ❸. Except for Venus and Uranus, they also rotate counter-clockwise on their axis ❹.

Planets travel around the Sun in an elliptical orbit; in other words, their path is slightly oval. Only Mercury and Pluto have orbits that are visibly oval.

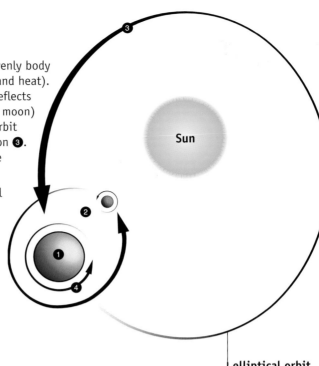

Sun

elliptical orbit

Despite the great number and variety of objects in the Solar System, it is almost empty. Most illustrations show the planets close together, but in fact vast empty spaces exist between them. The distances between the outer planets are even greater.

The **Oort Cloud**, made up of trillions of comets, orbits the Solar System at a distance of about 2,700 billion miles (4,500 billion km) from the Sun.

THE INNER PLANETS

The planets closest to the Sun are smaller and very dense; they are the rocky planets.

Mercury

Earth

Mars

Venus

The **asteroid belt**, which forms the border between the inner and outer planets, is the region of the Solar System where the most asteroids are found.

Comparative Table of the Planets

THE INNER PLANETS				
	Mercury	**Venus**	**Earth**	**Mars**
Diameter	3,029 mi (4,878 km)	7,514 mi (12,100 km)	7,921 mi (12,756 km)	4,215 mi (6,787 km)
Average distance from the Sun*	0.39 AU	0.72 AU	1 AU	1.52 AU
Rotation period	58.6 days	243 days	23.9 hrs.	24.6 hrs.
Revolution period	87.9 days	224.7 days	365.2 days	686.9 days
Orbital inclination (relative to the ecliptic)	7.0°	3.4°	0.0°	1.9°
Mass (relative to Earth)**	0.056	0.82	1	0.11
Number of known moons	0	0	1	2
Composition of atmosphere	trace of hydrogen and helium	96% CO_2, 3% nitrogen, 0.1% water	78% nitrogen, 21% oxygen, 1% argon	95% CO_2, 1.6% argon, 3% nitrogen

* 1 astronomical unit (AU) = 92,901,600 miles (149,600,000 km)

** Earth's mass = 6.5×10^{21} tons
   (5.9×10^{21} metric tons)

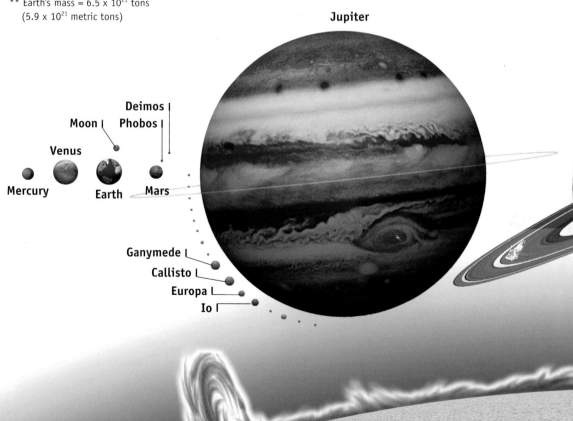

Jupiter

Deimos

Phobos

Moon

Venus

Mercury

Earth

Mars

Ganymede

Callisto

Europa

Io

Sun

THE OUTER PLANETS

Jupiter	Saturn	Uranus	Neptune	Pluto
88,793 mi (142,984 km)	74,853 mi (120,536 km)	31,738 mi (51,108 km)	30,763 mi (49,538 km)	1,410 mi (2,350 km)
5.2 AU	9.54 AU	19.19 AU	30.06 AU	39.44 AU
9.8 hrs.	10.6 hrs.	17.2 hrs.	16 hrs.	6.3 days
11.8 years	29.4 years	84 years	164.8 years	248.5 years
1.3°	2.5°	0.8°	1.8°	17.2°
318	95	15	17	0.002
17	22	21	8	1
90% hydrogen, 10% helium, traces of methane	96% hydrogen, 3% helium, 0.5% methane	84% hydrogen, 14% helium, 2% methane	74% hydrogen, 25% helium, 1% methane	methane and nitrogen

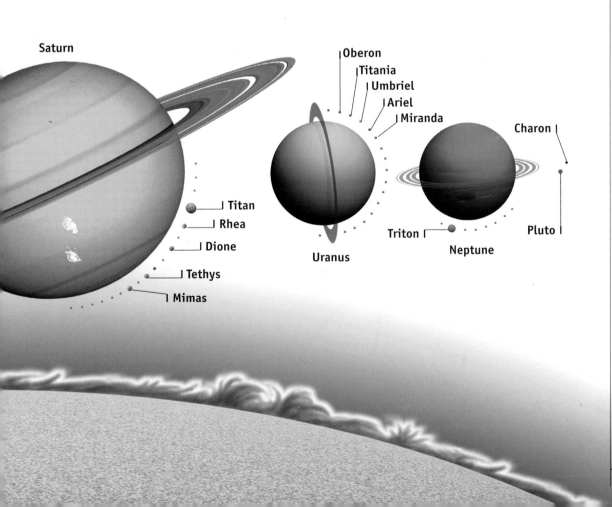

Saturn

Titan
Rhea
Dione
Tethys
Mimas

Oberon
Titania
Umbriel
Ariel
Miranda

Uranus

Triton

Neptune

Charon

Pluto

The Sun ☉

A very ordinary star

Located 92,901,600 miles (149,600,000 km) from Earth, the Sun is an average-sized yellow star, much like the hundred billion other stars in our galaxy. It is not a solid object, but a sphere of incandescent gas consisting mainly of hydrogen and helium.

Solar energy is produced at the center of the star, in its core ❶, where the temperature reaches 27,000,000° Fahrenheit (15,000,000° Celsius) and where hydrogen is converted into helium by means of nuclear fusion. In the radiative zone ❷, the energy produced migrates in the form of photons (light particles) and cools down. The photons interact constantly with solar matter, following such an irregular path ❸ that they take more than a million years to emerge from the radiative zone. They then cross the convection zone ❹, where whirls of hot gas ❺ circulate between the hotter lower regions and the "cooler" surface region. When they reach the photosphere ❻, the photons are emitted in the form of light and heat, at a temperature of 10,800° F (6,000° C). This light reaches Earth in eight minutes.

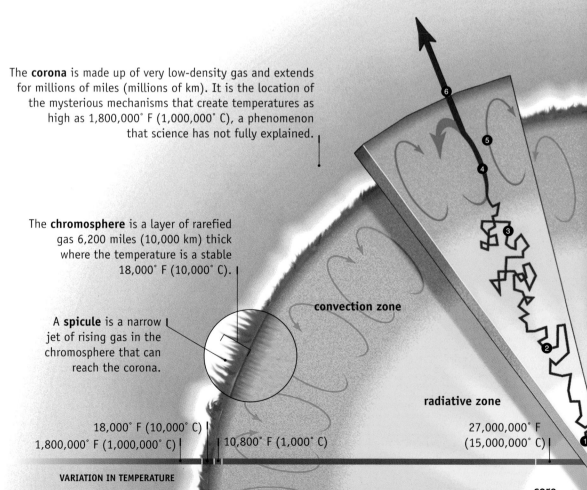

The **corona** is made up of very low-density gas and extends for millions of miles (millions of km). It is the location of the mysterious mechanisms that create temperatures as high as 1,800,000° F (1,000,000° C), a phenomenon that science has not fully explained.

The **chromosphere** is a layer of rarefied gas 6,200 miles (10,000 km) thick where the temperature is a stable 18,000° F (10,000° C).

A **spicule** is a narrow jet of rising gas in the chromosphere that can reach the corona.

convection zone

radiative zone

18,000° F (10,000° C)
1,800,000° F (1,000,000° C)

10,800° F (1,000° C)

27,000,000° F
(15,000,000° C)

VARIATION IN TEMPERATURE

core

SOLAR WIND

A permanent flow of protons and electrons moves away from the Sun at a speed of 310 miles (500 km) per second, reaching Earth in four days. This solar "wind" varies depending on the intensity of solar activity and affects the orientation of comet tails and polar auroras.

The corona is visible during a total solar eclipse, when it appears as a bright halo behind the Moon.

A computer-colored photograph of the Sun reveals the intensity of the solar wind.

SOLAR ACTIVITY

On Earth, the transmission of electricity and the signals transmitted by communications satellites are affected by phenomena known as magnetic storms, which are linked to fluctuations in the level of magnetic activity in the Sun. Every eleven years, the Sun goes through a period when sunspots and solar flares reach maximum levels before tapering off once again.

minimum activity

maximum activity

Sunspots are relatively cold (7,200° F [4,000° C]), dark regions of the photosphere where the magnetic field is very strong. Some sunspots cover areas five times as large as Earth's surface.

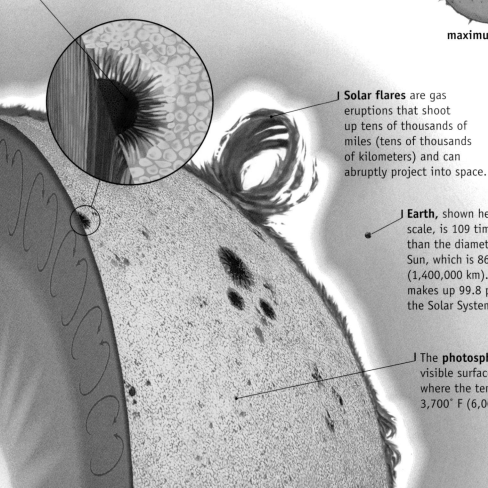

Solar flares are gas eruptions that shoot up tens of thousands of miles (tens of thousands of kilometers) and can abruptly project into space.

Earth, shown here in scale, is 109 times smaller than the diameter of the Sun, which is 869,400 miles (1,400,000 km). The Sun makes up 99.8 percent of the Solar System's mass.

The **photosphere** is the visible surface of the Sun, where the temperature is 3,700° F (6,000° C).

How the Sun Evolved

Our Sun: its birth and its fate

The Sun was born 4.6 billion years ago, or about 10 billion years after the Big Bang. It will take another 5 billion years or so to exhaust the fuel that drives its intense nuclear reactions, and it will shine for this entire time. In fact, over the next billion years, our star will grow brighter and our planet will become too hot to support life. We'll have to keep an eye on the situation!

❶ In one of the spiral arms of the Milky Way, a **dust cloud** began to gravitate due to the effect of a shock wave that was probably generated by the explosion of massive stars.

❷ In the center of this contracting cloud, the rotating matter became denser, hotter, and brighter, giving rise to an embryonic star, or **protostar.**

❸ The condensing matter caused a fantastic increase in temperature and triggered the nuclear reaction that made the Sun into a full-fledged star. Nearby dust agglomerated to form **protoplanets**.

❹ Lighter elements were repelled and formed the giant gaseous outer **planets**. Heavier elements conglomerated to make the rocky inner planets, including Earth.

❺ Four rocky planets (Mercury, Venus, Earth, and Mars), four giant gaseous planets (Jupiter, Saturn, Uranus, and Neptune), and a great number of other objects (asteroids, comets, and the planet Pluto) were formed to make up today's **Solar System.**

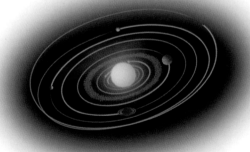

❻ Since that time, our star has been in a period of stability, and this has allowed life on Earth to develop. Scientists predict that over the next 500 million years the Sun will get bigger and brighter, raising the temperature on Earth so drastically that the oceans will evaporate.

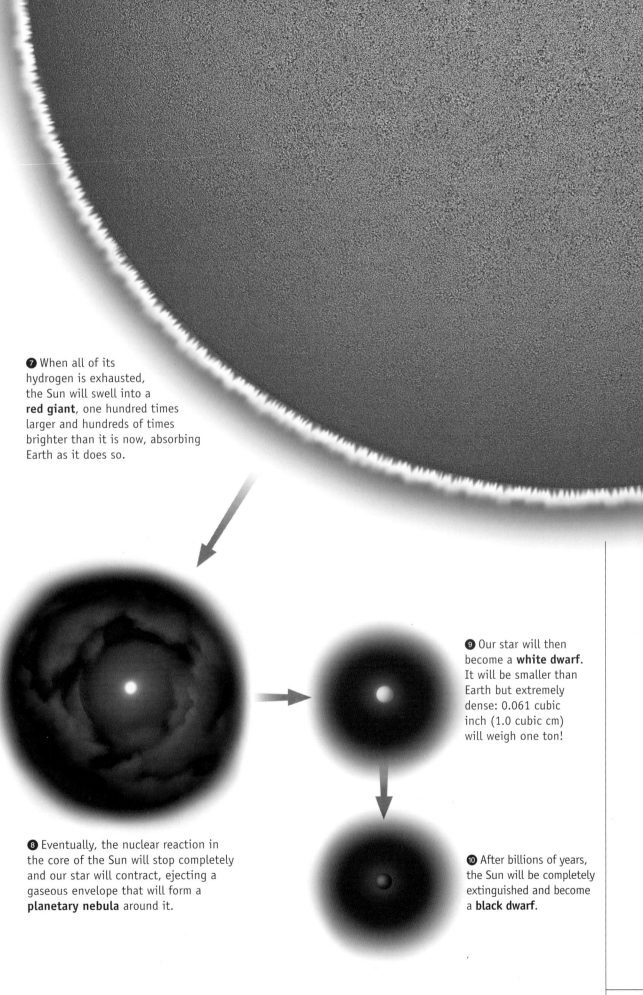

❼ When all of its hydrogen is exhausted, the Sun will swell into a **red giant**, one hundred times larger and hundreds of times brighter than it is now, absorbing Earth as it does so.

❽ Eventually, the nuclear reaction in the core of the Sun will stop completely and our star will contract, ejecting a gaseous envelope that will form a **planetary nebula** around it.

❾ Our star will then become a **white dwarf**. It will be smaller than Earth but extremely dense: 0.061 cubic inch (1.0 cubic cm) will weigh one ton!

❿ After billions of years, the Sun will be completely extinguished and become a **black dwarf**.

Solar Eclipses

A spectacular disappearing act

A solar eclipse takes place when, from Earth's perspective, the Moon passes in front of the Sun. In order for the eclipse to occur from Earth's vantage point, the three heavenly bodies must be perfectly aligned. Solar eclipses are the result of a remarkable coincidence that happens a limited number of times per century; nowhere else in the Solar System does such a perfect occultation of the Sun take place, since no other planet has a moon that can mask our star as completely.

Solar eclipses always happen during the day and are visible for only a few minutes at a time in small areas of the planet that are shaped like corridors several hundred miles (several hundred km) across.

TOTAL SOLAR ECLIPSE

A total solar eclipse lasts a maximum of seven minutes, during which time the solar corona is visible. Its umbra covers an area of more than 170 miles (270 km).

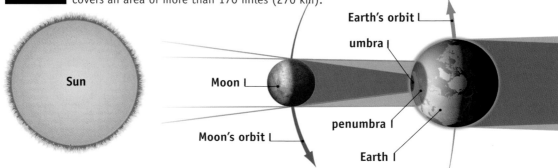

Earth's orbit

umbra

Sun

Moon

penumbra

Moon's orbit

Earth

ANNULAR ECLIPSE

An annular eclipse occurs when the Moon appears smaller than the Sun and leaves a ring of the solar disk showing. In this type of eclipse, the Moon is at its farthest point from Earth.

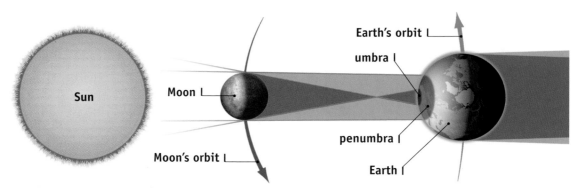

Earth's orbit

umbra

Sun

Moon

penumbra

Moon's orbit

Earth

PARTIAL ECLIPSE

Whenever a total or annular eclipse occurs, observers in a shadow zone, the penumbra, see a partial eclipse.

BE CAREFUL! DANGER!

Never, for any reason, look at the Sun with the naked eye. It seems easier to look at the Sun during a solar eclipse, but the devastating effect of infrared rays on the eyes remains the same. A safe way to observe an eclipse is to stand with the Sun behind you. Let the Sun's rays pass through a sheet of paper with a hole in it, and watch the eclipse on another sheet of paper.

Planets and Satellites

Even though the Sun contains 99.8 percent of the material in the Solar System and outshines, in every way, the nine planets that orbit it, the planets themselves are unique in many ways. What makes up our immediate neighbors, even the closest of which are millions of miles (millions of kilometers) away? What is it that makes Earth different from each of them? Exciting revelations about these seemingly familiar planets and their satellites await.

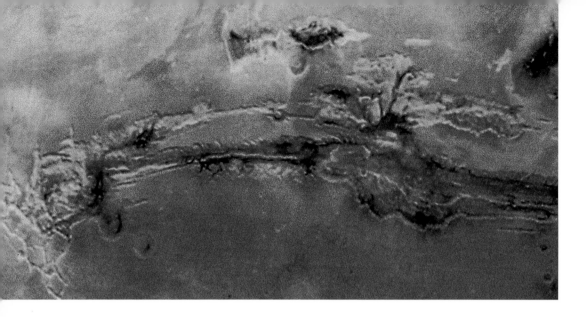

Planets and Satellites

Mercury ☿

The Sun's own moon

Mercury is the closest planet to the Sun and resembles the Moon, although it has a larger diameter (3,050 miles [4,900 km] versus 2,175 miles [3,500 km]). Like Earth's satellite, Mercury has no atmosphere, and its surface, which is several billion years old, is cratered. Ice might lie at the bottom of the polar craters, where the Sun's fiery rays never strike. Temperatures (-300° to 800° F [−185° to 425° C]) are the widest in the Solar System.

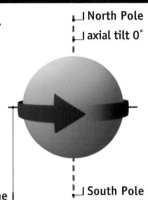

North Pole
axial tilt 0°
South Pole
orbital plane

MERCURY'S ORBIT

Mercury revolves around the Sun in a very eccentric orbit, with its closest point at 29 million miles (46 million km) and its farthest point at 43 million miles (70 million km).

The planet rotates one-and-a-half times on its axis during one revolution around the Sun.

crust

rock

After two revolutions, Mercury has completed three rotations. It is the only heavenly body in the Solar System synchronized in this way.

Almost 75 percent of the planet's diameter is composed of a large **core** of iron. The rocky matter that covers the core is almost as dense as terrestrial rock.

A RUGGED LANDSCAPE

crater

Mercury is crisscrossed by **ridges** a few thousand yards (meters) high, stretching for hundreds of miles (hundreds of km) and running across craters. The ridges were apparently formed by the cooling of the planet's core, which compressed, buckled, and creased the crust.

Venus ♀

Venus has long been considered to have the most features in common with Earth. It is almost the same size; it has a thick atmosphere; and it has the same density and chemical composition. Only a few decades ago, it was thought to be covered with dense vegetation. Unfortunately, conditions on Venus were found to be inhospitable to life.

North Pole
axial tilt 2°

orbital plane

South Pole

Venus rotates clockwise, unlike all other bodies in the Solar System.

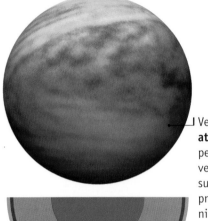

Venus' opaque **atmosphere** permanently veils the planet's surface. The pressure is ninety times that on Earth.

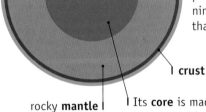

rocky **mantle**

crust

Its **core** is made of iron and nickel.

THE SURFACE OF VENUS

In addition to the fairly flat hilly plains that form its landscape as a whole, Venus has huge volcanoes resembling those in the Hawaiian archipelago.

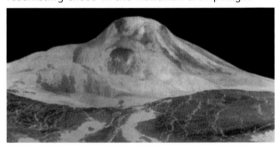

The planet is covered with lava flows and has mountains such as **Maat Mons**, which is 5 miles (8 km) high.

THE GREENHOUSE EFFECT

The atmosphere, made of 96 percent carbon dioxide (CO_2), traps most of the solar energy and produces a severe greenhouse effect. The temperature at the surface reaches 870° F (465° C).

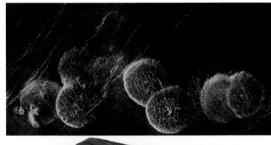

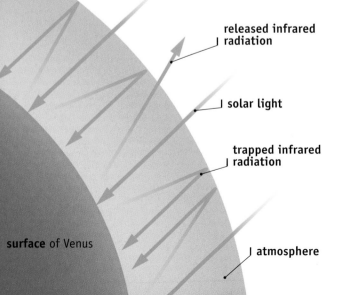

released infrared radiation

solar light

trapped infrared radiation

surface of Venus

atmosphere

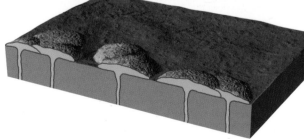

Venus reveals stunning geological structures in the form of collapsed **domes** resulting from the expulsion, then retraction, of lava.

Earth ⊕

Inside a rocky planet

Earth is one of the Solar System's rocky planets. Each cubic yard (0.76 cubic m) of Earth weighs about 4 tons (3.5 metric tons), making it the densest body in the Solar System. It is also the only planet with vast liquid oceans.

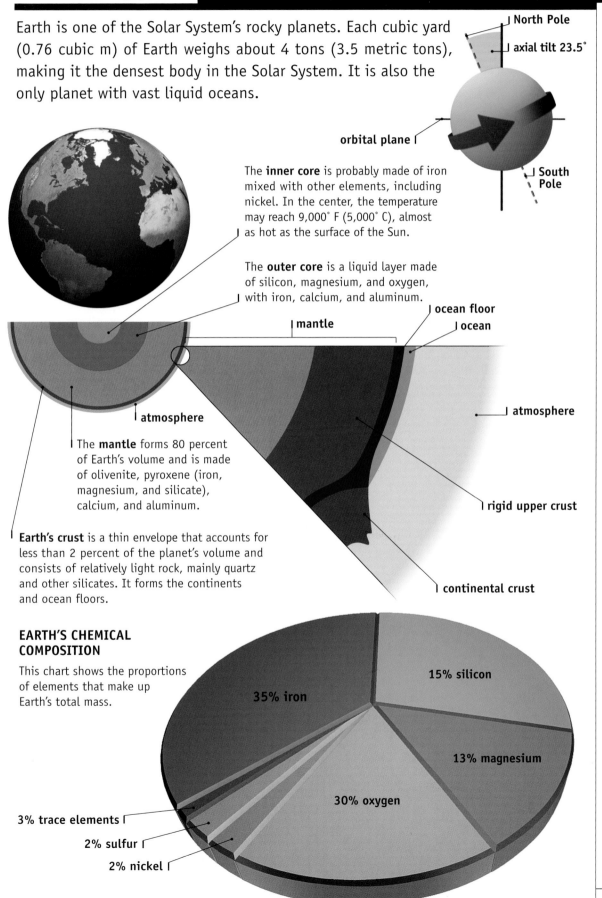

North Pole

axial tilt 23.5°

orbital plane

South Pole

The **inner core** is probably made of iron mixed with other elements, including nickel. In the center, the temperature may reach 9,000° F (5,000° C), almost as hot as the surface of the Sun.

The **outer core** is a liquid layer made of silicon, magnesium, and oxygen, with iron, calcium, and aluminum.

ocean floor

ocean

mantle

atmosphere

atmosphere

The **mantle** forms 80 percent of Earth's volume and is made of olivenite, pyroxene (iron, magnesium, and silicate), calcium, and aluminum.

rigid upper crust

Earth's crust is a thin envelope that accounts for less than 2 percent of the planet's volume and consists of relatively light rock, mainly quartz and other silicates. It forms the continents and ocean floors.

continental crust

EARTH'S CHEMICAL COMPOSITION

This chart shows the proportions of elements that make up Earth's total mass.

35% iron

15% silicon

13% magnesium

30% oxygen

3% trace elements

2% sulfur

2% nickel

How Was Earth Born?

The formation and evolution of our planet

Five billion years ago, the Solar System did not exist. There was only a huge, diffuse cloud of dust and gas turning slowly on itself. The nine planets, including Earth, were formed by the agglomeration of matter, a little like a snowball, within this original nebula.

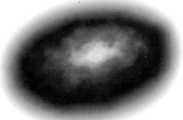  

❶ The process began some 4.6 billion years ago, near the center of the **solar nebula**.

❷ The **Sun** formed in the center of this cloud, while the gases and matter on the periphery began to agglomerate.

❸ Small pebbles grew larger, forming embryonic planets, or **protoplanets**, a few miles (a few km) in diameter.

❹ The protoplanets collided with each other and agglomerated until they reached the size of **planets** several thousand miles (several thousand km) in diameter. Over hundreds of millions of years, the emerging planets were intensely bombarded by other rocky bodies.

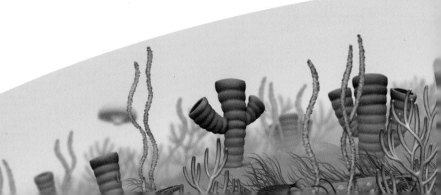

❺ About 4.5 billion years ago, the young Earth was completely covered with a **sea of burning lava** — liquid rock — several hundred miles (several hundred km) thick.

❻ Slowly, the sea of lava cooled to form a **crust**, which continued to be subjected to intense bombardment by meteorites and comets.

❼ Our young planet also experienced volcanic activity, which liberated an early **atmosphere** radically different from that of the present day. Water also appeared — perhaps from the depths of Earth or brought from space by comets — and formed oceans. At the same time, the crust shifted, creating continents.

❽ The presence of continents, oceans, and an oxygen-poor atmosphere resulted in the formation of more and more complex molecules, which led to a remarkable phenomenon: **life**. Even more surprising, life appeared quickly in the oceans, less than one billion years after Earth was born. It took several billion years to extend onto land, however.

The Magnetosphere

A shield against the solar wind

Like other heavenly bodies, including most planets and the Sun, Earth is a sort of giant magnet. Its magnetic field, the magnetosphere, acts as a shield, protecting us by deflecting most of the nuclear particles that come from the Sun, which are dangerous to all forms of life.

The solar wind ❶, a permanent flow of particles whose intensity varies depending on the Sun's activity, reaches Earth at a velocity of 190 to 500 miles (300 to 800 km) per second. It forms a shock wave ❷ when it meets Earth's magnetic field. Most of the particles are deflected to a zone called the magnetosheath ❸. Some, however, are trapped in the inner and outer Van Allen belts ❹. Others sometimes penetrate the upper atmosphere via the polar horns ❺ and create auroral lights.

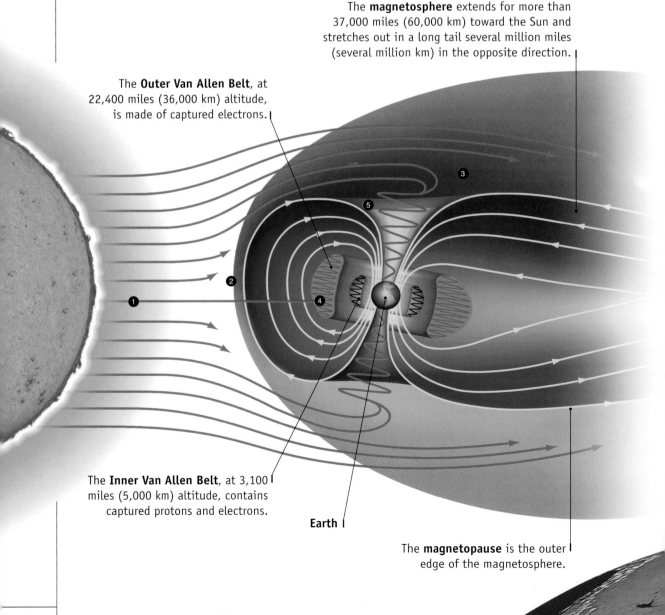

The **magnetosphere** extends for more than 37,000 miles (60,000 km) toward the Sun and stretches out in a long tail several million miles (several million km) in the opposite direction.

The **Outer Van Allen Belt**, at 22,400 miles (36,000 km) altitude, is made of captured electrons.

The **Inner Van Allen Belt**, at 3,100 miles (5,000 km) altitude, contains captured protons and electrons.

Earth

The **magnetopause** is the outer edge of the magnetosphere.

MARVELOUS POLAR LIGHTS

Only recently has physics solved the mystery of auroral lights. This phenomenon is produced when certain nuclear particles from the solar wind penetrate the upper atmosphere (the ionosphere) through the polar horns. When they collide with the atoms and molecules of the upper atmosphere, these particles produce spectacular light displays. In the north, they are called the aurora borealis; in the south, the aurora australis. They extend over thousands of miles (thousands of km) but are less than 0.5 mile (1 km) thick.

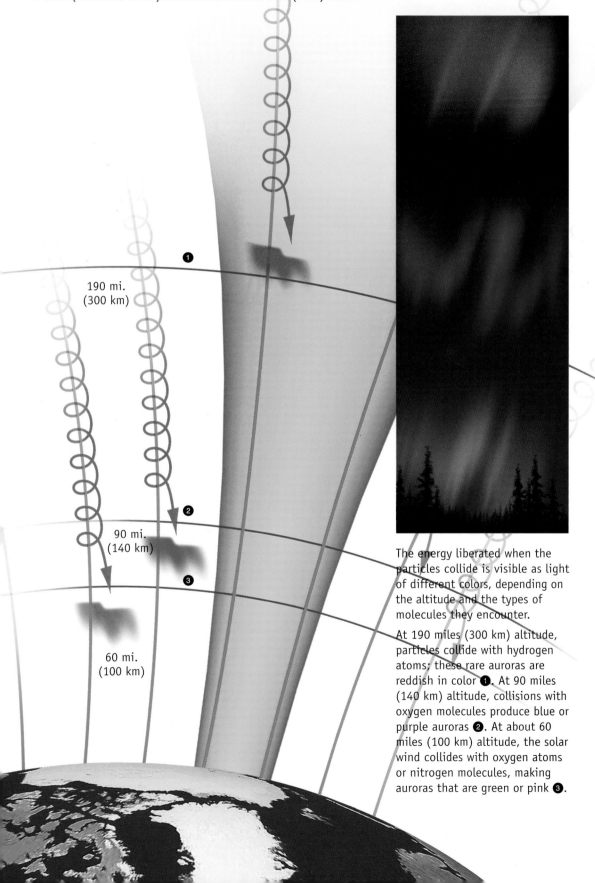

❶

190 mi. (300 km)

❷

90 mi. (140 km)

❸

60 mi. (100 km)

The energy liberated when the particles collide is visible as light of different colors, depending on the altitude and the types of molecules they encounter.

At 190 miles (300 km) altitude, particles collide with hydrogen atoms; these rare auroras are reddish in color ❶. At 90 miles (140 km) altitude, collisions with oxygen molecules produce blue or purple auroras ❷. At about 60 miles (100 km) altitude, the solar wind collides with oxygen atoms or nitrogen molecules, making auroras that are green or pink ❸.

Earth's Atmosphere

A thin, precious layer of air

Earth is nicknamed "the blue planet" largely because its atmosphere makes it possible for oceans to exist. Without an atmosphere, our planet would look like the Moon or Mars, with no liquid water.

A thin layer of air, containing a good proportion of free oxygen, protects us from the Sun's harmful rays and makes life on Earth possible.

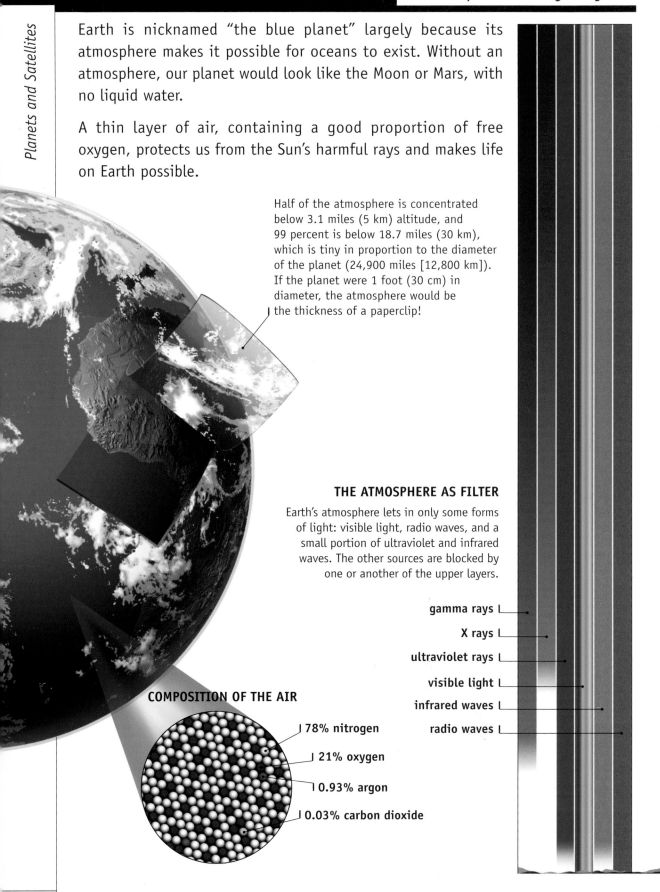

Half of the atmosphere is concentrated below 3.1 miles (5 km) altitude, and 99 percent is below 18.7 miles (30 km), which is tiny in proportion to the diameter of the planet (24,900 miles [12,800 km]). If the planet were 1 foot (30 cm) in diameter, the atmosphere would be the thickness of a paperclip!

THE ATMOSPHERE AS FILTER

Earth's atmosphere lets in only some forms of light: visible light, radio waves, and a small portion of ultraviolet and infrared waves. The other sources are blocked by one or another of the upper layers.

gamma rays
X rays
ultraviolet rays
visible light
infrared waves
radio waves

COMPOSITION OF THE AIR

78% nitrogen

21% oxygen

0.93% argon

0.03% carbon dioxide

THE LAYERS OF THE ATMOSPHERE

The atmosphere is made up of several layers, extending from the troposphere, in which we live, to the exosphere, the outermost layer. Each layer has different characteristics.

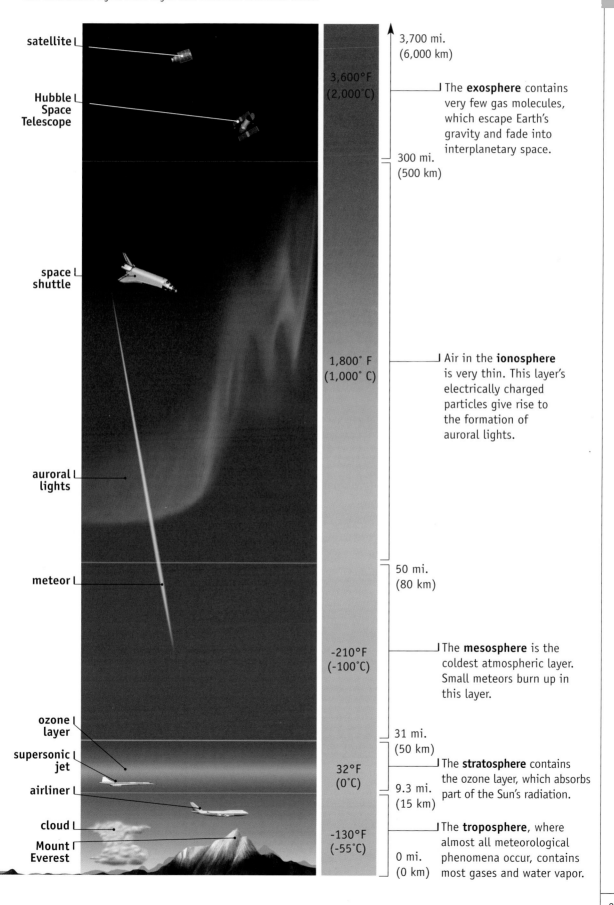

satellite

Hubble Space Telescope

space shuttle

auroral lights

meteor

ozone layer

supersonic jet

airliner

cloud

Mount Everest

3,700 mi. (6,000 km)

3,600°F (2,000°C)

The **exosphere** contains very few gas molecules, which escape Earth's gravity and fade into interplanetary space.

300 mi. (500 km)

1,800° F (1,000° C)

Air in the **ionosphere** is very thin. This layer's electrically charged particles give rise to the formation of auroral lights.

50 mi. (80 km)

-210°F (-100°C)

The **mesosphere** is the coldest atmospheric layer. Small meteors burn up in this layer.

31 mi. (50 km)

32°F (0°C)

The **stratosphere** contains the ozone layer, which absorbs part of the Sun's radiation.

9.3 mi. (15 km)

-130°F (-55°C)

The **troposphere**, where almost all meteorological phenomena occur, contains most gases and water vapor.

0 mi. (0 km)

Geographic Coordinates

Getting one's bearings on Earth

A simple system of geographic coordinates has been devised to locate places on Earth. This system uses intersecting horizontal and vertical lines to identify any point accurately. We locate a geographic point using two coordinates, longitude (meridians) and latitude (parallels), which are expressed in degrees.

THE MERIDIANS

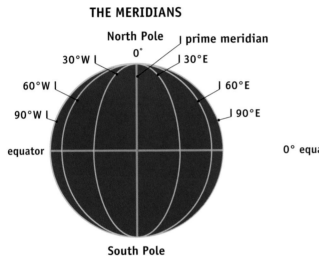

THE PARALLELS

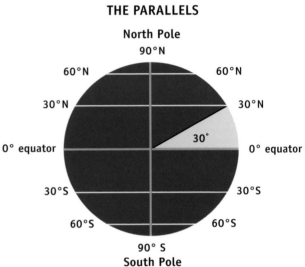

Meridians are imaginary lines that run perpendicular to the equator and meet at the poles. These semi-circles divide Earth into sections resembling parts of an orange. From the zero, or prime, meridian, we divide the globe into two hemispheres: east and west, each of which is subdivided into 180 degrees.

Imaginary horizontal lines, parallel to the equator, circle Earth. The lines are shorter closer to the poles. The equator divides the globe into two hemispheres, north and south, so a 30th parallel runs in the north and in the south. The angle at the equator is 0°, and the maximum angle is 90° at the poles.

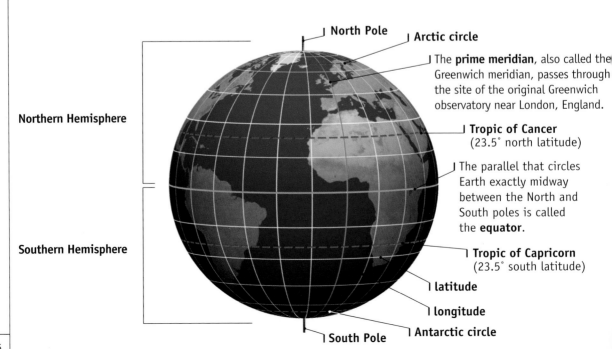

North Pole

Arctic circle

The **prime meridian**, also called the Greenwich meridian, passes through the site of the original Greenwich observatory near London, England.

Northern Hemisphere

Tropic of Cancer (23.5° north latitude)

The parallel that circles Earth exactly midway between the North and South poles is called the **equator**.

Southern Hemisphere

Tropic of Capricorn (23.5° south latitude)

latitude

longitude

Antarctic circle

South Pole

Astronomical Coordinates

Finding objects in the sky

To make locating stars easier, we use a system of horizontal and vertical lines similar to those used in geographical coordinates. The same principles apply: there are celestial poles, a celestial equator, and northern and southern hemispheres. To avoid confusion with latitudes and longitudes, these are called, respectively, declinations (the parallels) and right ascensions (the meridians).

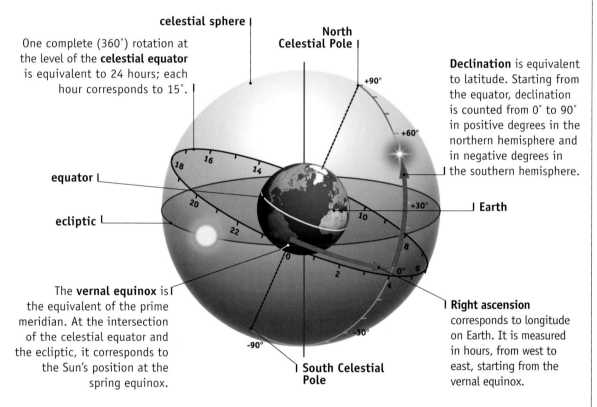

celestial sphere

One complete (360°) rotation at the level of the **celestial equator** is equivalent to 24 hours; each hour corresponds to 15°.

North Celestial Pole

equator

ecliptic

Declination is equivalent to latitude. Starting from the equator, declination is counted from 0° to 90° in positive degrees in the northern hemisphere and in negative degrees in the southern hemisphere.

Earth

The **vernal equinox** is the equivalent of the prime meridian. At the intersection of the celestial equator and the ecliptic, it corresponds to the Sun's position at the spring equinox.

Right ascension corresponds to longitude on Earth. It is measured in hours, from west to east, starting from the vernal equinox.

South Celestial Pole

EARTH IS TURNING

When we observe the sky, it seems that the stars are moving from east to west, but in reality it is Earth that is rotating from west to east. The point at which observers are located on Earth determines which stars they see and the direction in which those stars seem to be moving.

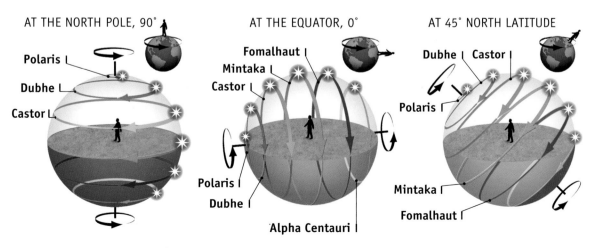

AT THE NORTH POLE, 90°

Polaris
Dubhe
Castor

AT THE EQUATOR, 0°

Fomalhaut
Mintaka
Castor

Polaris
Dubhe

Alpha Centauri

AT 45° NORTH LATITUDE

Dubhe | Castor

Polaris

Mintaka

Fomalhaut

The Seasons

Why weather is cyclical

Contrary to popular belief, the seasons — the gradual changes in climatic conditions over the months — do not occur because Earth gets closer to or farther away from the Sun. Seasonal climatic variations are caused by the slight inclination of Earth, which rotates around its axis like a top that leans at an angle of 23.5 degrees. It is because of this axial tilt that one hemisphere receives more Sun than the other at a given time of year.

If the axis of the poles were not tilted, there would be no seasonal variations in temperature. Our climate would be more or less like what we experience in October and March. In fact, Mercury and Venus have no axial tilt.

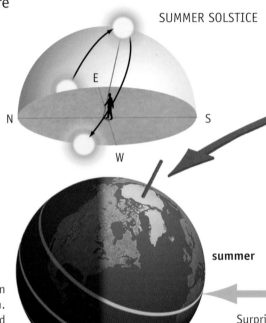

SUMMER SOLSTICE

summer

In summer, the Sun is high in the sky and the weather is warm. The **summer solstice**, around June 21, is the longest day of the year in the northern hemisphere.

Surprisingly, in the northern hemisphere the hot season takes place when Earth is at its maximum distance from the Sun, its **aphelion**, 94.5 million miles (152.1 million km) away.

ANGLE OF INCIDENCE OF THE SUN'S RAYS

The difference in temperatures in various regions of the globe results from the Earth's inclination with regard to the Sun and is explained by the angle of incidence of the Sun's rays.

At the North Pole, the Sun's rays are almost parallel to the surface. Their energy is dissipated; it is cold.

In the northern hemisphere, the Sun's rays hit the ground at an angle. Their energy is spread over a surface three times larger than at the equator, and it is therefore less concentrated. The climate is temperate.

At the equator, the Sun's rays are concentrated and hit the surface of the ground at a 90° angle; it is hot.

VERNAL EQUINOX

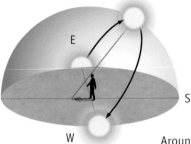

E

N — S

W

spring

Around March 21, day and night are the same length; this is the **vernal equinox**. On this day, the Sun rises exactly in the east and sets exactly in the west.

WINTER SOLSTICE

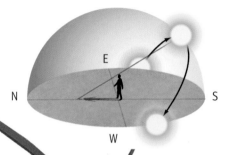

E

N — S

W

winter

Sun

In the northern hemisphere, the cold season takes place when Earth is closest to the Sun, at its **perihelion**, 91.5 million miles (147.3 million km) away.

In winter, the Sun is low in the sky and the weather is cold. The **winter solstice**, around December 21, is the shortest day of the year in the northern hemisphere.

AUTUMNAL EQUINOX

E

N — S

W

Around September 21, day and night are the same length; this is called the **autumnal equinox**. On this day, the Sun rises exactly in the east and sets exactly in the west.

autumn

The Moon ☽

The Moon has all the attributes of a planet, since its size (one-quarter that of Earth), its surface, and its history are comparable to those of planets close to the Sun. It is considered a natural satellite, however, because it revolves around Earth. The Moon has no atmosphere or water, but the lunar poles may likely have some ice mixed with grit at the bottom of the polar craters, where the temperature is always below −325° F (-200° C). Under these extreme conditions, this mixture forms a material as hard as rock.

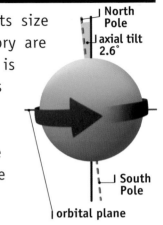

North Pole

axial tilt 2.6°

South Pole

orbital plane

near side

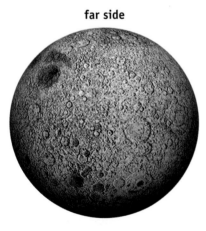

The **surface of the Moon** is extremely rugged; it has craters several hundred miles (several hundred km) in diameter, mountains 5.6 miles (9 km) high, and ravines 3.7 miles (6 km) deep.

The **maria (seas)**, vast plains of solidified lava, form dark regions that can be seen with the naked eye.

far side

The **bright rays** from ejected matter spread over several hundred miles (several hundred km) from young craters.

crater range

The ferrous **inner core** has a temperature of 2200° F (1200° C).

The **outer core** is viscous.

The solid **mantle** is 620 miles (1,000 km) thick.

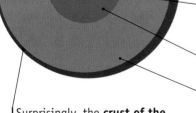

Surprisingly, the **crust of the Moon** is thinner on the near side (40 miles [60 km]) than on the far side (60 miles [100 km]).

An astronaut's footprint on the Moon's surface shows the regolith, or surface dust.

A COSMIC COLLISION

It is thought that the Moon was born from a catastrophic collision between Earth and a huge asteroid ❶. The impact propelled into space enormous quantities of matter from Earth and the destroyed object ❷. Under Earth's gravity, the debris began to orbit Earth ❸ and became amalgamated ❹ to form the Moon ❺.

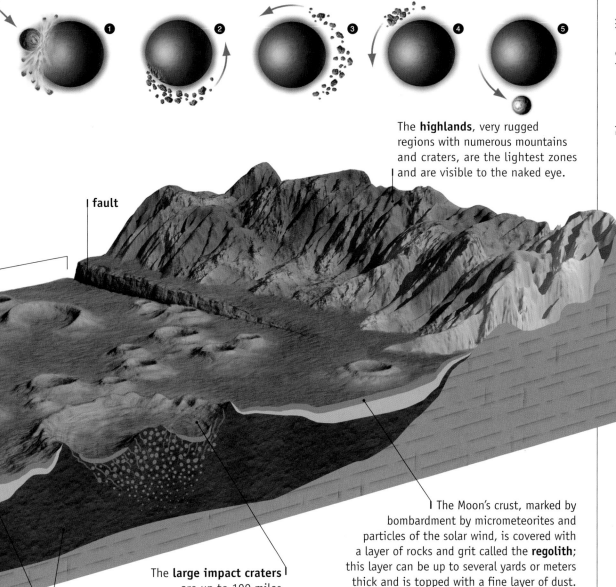

The **highlands**, very rugged regions with numerous mountains and craters, are the lightest zones and are visible to the naked eye.

fault

The **large impact craters** are up to 190 miles (300 km) in diameter.

layers of lava

The Moon's crust, marked by bombardment by micrometeorites and particles of the solar wind, is covered with a layer of rocks and grit called the **regolith**; this layer can be up to several yards or meters thick and is topped with a fine layer of dust.

ROCKS SEVERAL BILLION YEARS OLD

Many lunar rocks have been brought back to Earth for analysis. These samples, which can be dated, are an important source of information.

Anorthosite is a component of the highlands. It is generally more than 4 billion years old.

Basalt is volcanic rock riddled with holes from gas bubbles; it is found in great quantity in the maria. It is between 3.2 and 3.8 billion years old.

Breccia consists of fragments of rock that became cemented together following meteoric impacts.

Lunar Phases

Why the Moon changes shape

Each month, the Moon changes in appearance, waxing from a thin crescent to a half Moon to a full Moon, then waning in the same way. This is the result of the Moon's movement in relation to the Sun, as seen from Earth. Since the Moon shines by reflecting solar light, its phases result from its position relative to Earth and the Sun.

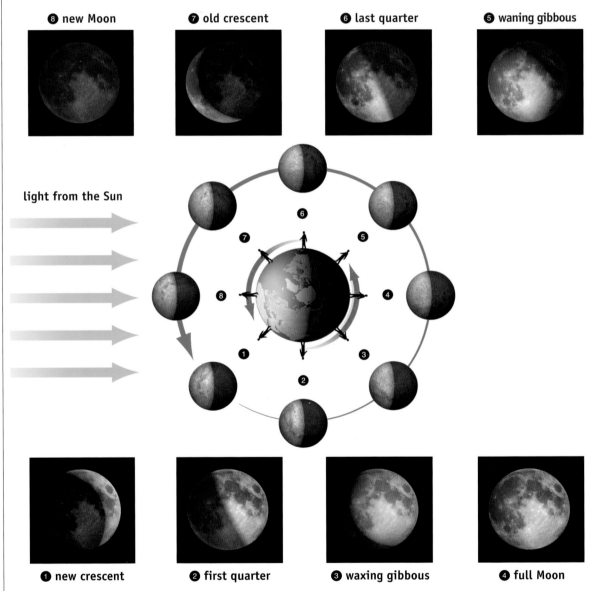

❽ new Moon   **❼ old crescent**   **❻ last quarter**   **❺ waning gibbous**

light from the Sun

❶ new crescent   **❷ first quarter**   **❸ waxing gibbous**   **❹ full Moon**

At the beginning of the lunar cycle, the Moon looks like a thin crescent. It is to the left of the Sun in the sky and visible in the early evening ❶. Every night, more of its near side is lit and the lunar crescent thickens. After one week, it has become a half Moon ❷. The Moon continues to move away from the Sun ❸. When the Moon is full, its entire near side is lit; seen from Earth, the Sun seems to shine directly on it ❹.

Then the reverse process begins. As the Moon begins to draw closer to the Sun in the sky, shadow spreads across its face ❺. Night after night, the lit portion recedes until there is a half Moon ❻. Soon after, the Moon is to the right of the Sun and appears in the sky at dawn, as a thin crescent ❼. Finally, the Moon disappears completely. This is the new Moon. It is present in the sky but invisible, as light from the Sun blots it out ❽.

Lunar Eclipses

When the Moon turns red

We can watch lunar eclipses, unlike solar eclipses, without harming our eyes. Although they are less spectacular, they occur more frequently and last longer. A lunar eclipse takes place when Earth comes between the Moon and the Sun and the three bodies are aligned. Because Earth's diameter is four times the size of the Moon's, the Moon is shaded totally for one hour in the umbra cast by Earth.

Earth's atmosphere refracts a small amount of the Sun's light toward the inside of the umbra, making the Moon appear red.

A lunar eclipse starts when the Moon enters the penumbra; its luminosity diminishes almost imperceptibly. It then enters the umbra, where part of its disk is darkened; this is a partial lunar eclipse ❶. When it is completely in the umbra, the Moon takes on a pronounced red tinge; this is a total lunar eclipse ❷.

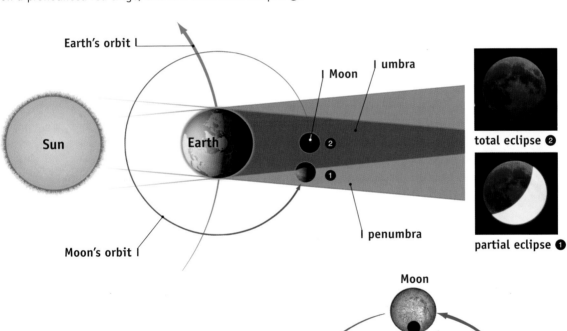

Earth's orbit

Moon

umbra

Sun

Earth

Moon's orbit

penumbra

total eclipse ❷

partial eclipse ❶

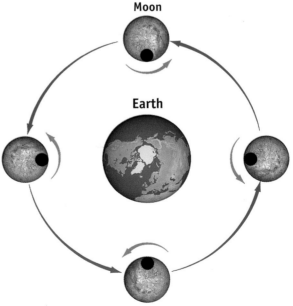

Moon

Earth

ONE SIDE IN SIGHT

We always see the same side of the Moon because our satellite takes exactly the same amount of time to rotate on its axis as it does to revolve around Earth: twenty-seven days and eight hours. This is why one side can never be seen from Earth.

Mars ♂

The fascinating Red Planet

Of all planets in the Solar System, Mars has always been the most fascinating. Half the size of Earth, it has almost all of the conditions needed for life: an atmosphere, a temperate climate, and water at the poles (and probably underground). According to what we currently know, Mars is the only planet on which we might some day live.

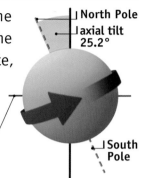

North Pole
axial tilt 25.2°
South Pole
orbital plane

Mars' **inclination** is almost identical to Earth's. The Red Planet has seasons comparable to ours, but they are twice as long because it takes 687 days for Mars to revolve around the Sun.

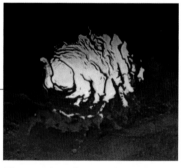

THE MARTIAN MOONS

Mars has two tiny moons called **Phobos** ("fear") and **Deimos** ("terror"), which look more like large rocks. They are probably asteroids from the nearby asteroid belt that were captured by the planet's gravity.

ferrous **core**

rocky **mantle**

The **south polar cap** is composed of sand, frozen carbon dioxide, and ice. The polar caps shrink and grow with the seasons, as they do on Earth.

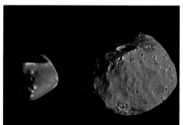

Mars' **crust** contains iron oxide, which gives it its red color. The atmosphere is pink for the same reason. In short, Mars is a rusty planet.

THE WILDEST LANDSCAPE IN THE SOLAR SYSTEM

The highest known mountain, **Olympus Mons**, is a huge volcano 16.8 miles (27 km) high (three times the height of Mount Everest) and 370 miles (600 km) in diameter.

The biggest canyon, **Valles Marineris**, is more than 2,480 miles (4,000 km) long (the width of the United States) and has escarpments 3 to 6 miles (5 to 10 km) deep.

The Asteroids

Small, unexplored planets

Asteroids are small bodies made of rock and metal that revolve around the Sun as the planets do. They are small, usually less than 60 miles (100 km) in diameter. Unlike planets, asteroids are not spherical in shape; instead, they are irregularly shaped, very dark-colored rocks. Some, such as the Martian moons (Phobos and Deimos) and some of Jupiter's small moons, may have been captured by planets.

Most asteroids have a nearly circular orbit around the Sun; Ceres is one of these ❶. But some asteroids, such as Icarus ❷ and Apollo ❸ have very eccentric orbits that cross Earth's orbit. It is estimated that hundreds, or even thousands, of these Earth-crossing asteroids exist, and some of them may collide with our planet one day.

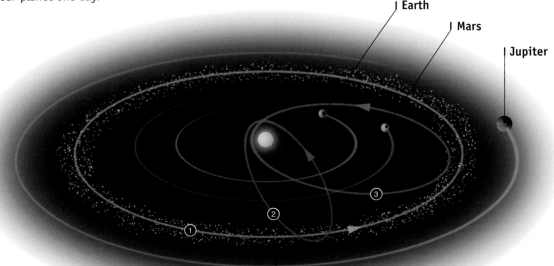

| Earth
| Mars
| Jupiter

A large number of asteroids revolve around the Sun in the **asteroid belt** between the orbits of Mars and Jupiter. Their total mass is less than the Moon's.

THOUSANDS OF ASTEROIDS

We know that there are hundreds of thousands of asteroids. More than seven thousand asteroids are known, and every year more are discovered. Each receives a name and an official number corresponding to the chronological order of its discovery (1 Ceres, 2 Pallas, 3 Juno, 4 Vesta, etc.).

Ida, discovered by the *Galileo* probe in 1993, is 32 miles (52 km) long and has a tiny moon, **Dactyl.**

Gaspra was photographed by the *Galileo* probe in 1991; it is 12 miles (20 km) long and has craters on its surface.

Toutatis, named in honor of the god of the Gauls who feared that the sky would fall on their heads, may pass close to Earth in September 2004.

The largest asteroid, **Ceres**, discovered in 1801, is more than 620 miles (1,000 km) in diameter. Its mass equals one-quarter of the mass of all other asteroids combined.

Meteorites

Stones that fall from the sky

Earth is constantly bombarded by rocky particles that come from the asteroid belt between Mars and Jupiter. Drawn by Earth's gravity, these particles fall into our atmosphere at breakneck speed. Every day, hundreds of tons of cosmic matter reach our planet!

We call these space-borne fragments of rock and particles of dust **meteoroids**. Although most burn up before they reach the ground, some do reach Earth's surface.

When meteoroids penetrate the atmosphere, they form a short, luminous streak made of the main fragment and a tail of incandescent debris. A common name for them is **falling stars** (although they are not stars); science calls them **meteors**. These grains of dust are about the size of a pinhead.

FALLING TO EARTH

A meteor that does not burn up as it passes through the atmosphere becomes a **meteorite**. Traces of meteorites weighing from a few ounces or grams to several tons have been found on Earth.

When it hits the ground, the meteorite partially disintegrates and creates a **shock wave** that moves through Earth's crust. Upon impact, an **explosion** occurs and debris is scattered over several miles (several km).

The meteorite, hitting Earth at great speed, forms a **crater** with raised sides ten to twenty times bigger than the meteorite itself.

HUGE IMPACTS LEAVE THEIR MARK

Many scientists believe that in the past, large meteorites striking Earth caused the extinction of at least 90 percent of life on the planet. Today, a major collision seems highly unlikely. About one hundred large-impact craters have been found throughout the world, but Earth has no doubt been struck by many more meteorites. Scientists estimated that two-thirds of the meteorites that reach the planet's surface are lost forever because two-thirds of the globe is covered with water.

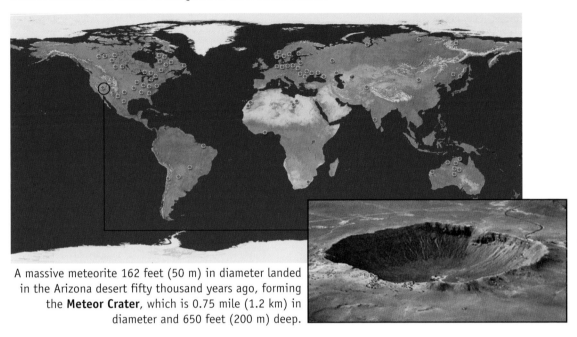

A massive meteorite 162 feet (50 m) in diameter landed in the Arizona desert fifty thousand years ago, forming the **Meteor Crater**, which is 0.75 mile (1.2 km) in diameter and 650 feet (200 m) deep.

TYPES OF METEORITES

Over the past two centuries, several thousand meteorites have been found offering samples of the Solar System that are of enormous scientific value. Many meteorites have been preserved in the Antarctic, where they are easy to collect because the fragments contrast well against the snow. Generally, three types of meteorites exist.

Stony-iron meteorites are made of iron and rocky matter.

Iron meteorites are made mainly of iron and nickel.

The composition of **stony** meteorites resembles that of Earth's mantle and crust. They are divided into two categories:

Chondrite meteorites seem to be the most common. They are probably the oldest in the Solar System.

Achondrite meteorites are similar to terrestrial basalt and come from the Moon and Mars.

Comets

Beacons of terror or luck?

Planets and Satellites

Comets are tiny objects that should be very difficult to see. And yet, thanks to a spectacular visual effect, they are the only planetoids known since ancient times. When a comet approaches the Sun, it begins to vaporize. The stream of vaporized matter reflects light from the Sun, and a magnificent tail stretching millions of miles (millions of km) spreads out behind the comet. We now know that comets crash into planets, something that has certainly happened on Earth many times. As significant sources of organic matter and water, they may have played a role in the development of the oceans and life on our planet. Comets are different from asteroids because they are made mainly of ice and grit; scientists generally think of them as dirty snowballs.

A **hydrogen cloud**, a huge envelope several million miles (several million km) across, surrounds the comet.

The **dust tail**, made of extremely fine particles, can be more than 6 million miles (10 million km) long. This is the spectacular tail that we see in the sky.

The materials that surround the nucleus are transformed from solids into gases due to heat. They form the **coma**, which is composed of water, carbon dioxide, and various gases.

THE ORIGIN OF COMETS

Comets come from the Oort Cloud on the outer edges of the Solar System. The Oort Cloud contains trillions of comets. From time to time, a comet separates from the cloud and plunges toward the Sun.

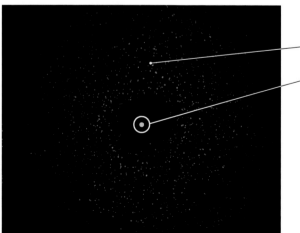

Oort Cloud

Solar System

The **nucleus**, in the center, is made of gas and rocky dust and remains relatively solid and stable. Some of this material is emitted from the crust of the nucleus when the comet passes close to the Sun.

The **ion tail**, which can be up to 60 million miles (100 million km) long, is formed of ionized gases that interact with the solar wind.

Some comets have a highly elliptical orbit. This is true of the famous Halley's Comet.

THE COMETS' ORBITS

Scientists have plotted the orbits of about 900 comets. Some have an orbit between the paths of Venus and Mars and take just several years to complete a revolution. Others have very eccentric orbits — shaped like very elongated ovals — that take decades, or even many centuries, to complete.

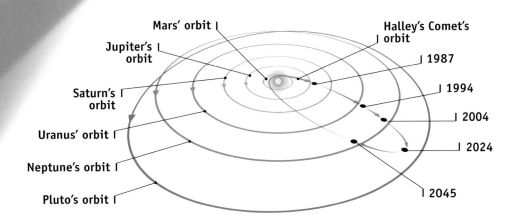

Mars' orbit

Jupiter's orbit

Saturn's orbit

Uranus' orbit

Neptune's orbit

Pluto's orbit

Halley's Comet's orbit

1987

1994

2004

2024

2045

A COMET STRIKES

It is fairly rare for a comet to hit a planet; this happened in July 1994, when the **Shoemaker-Levy 9** comet broke into some 20 fragments and hit Jupiter.

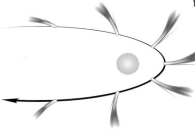

The cascade of collisions with the Shoemaker-Levy 9 comet left Jupiter's atmosphere with dark **spots** larger than Earth. These spots lasted for months.

A comet's tail always points away from the Sun, since it is caused by the solar wind blowing on the cloud of gas surrounding the comet. When the comet approaches the Sun, its tail stretches out behind it.

Jupiter ♃

The giant planet

The largest planet in the Solar System is 1,400 times the size of Earth, and its mass is 2.5 times that of all of the other planets combined. Jupiter could almost have become a star, since its elements are similar to the Sun's: 90 percent hydrogen and 10 percent helium, with traces of methane, water, ammonia, and rocky dust. But it would have had to be bigger in order for a thermonuclear reaction to be triggered.

North Pole
axial tilt
3.1°

South Pole

orbital plane

Jupiter is one of the four giant gaseous planets with no solid **surface**. Its matter becomes denser as it descends through the gaseous atmosphere toward the center.

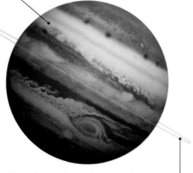

The planet has three or four very **faint**, almost invisible rings made up of fine dark particles.

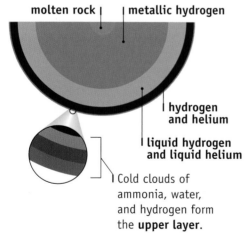

molten rock | metallic hydrogen

hydrogen and helium

liquid hydrogen and liquid helium

Cold clouds of ammonia, water, and hydrogen form the **upper layer**.

JUPITER'S NATURAL SATELLITES

In a sort of mirror image of the Sun, Jupiter is surrounded by a mini-solar system made up of eight moons that we know of. The four largest moons — Io, Europa, Ganymede, and Callisto — are as big as planets such as Mars, Mercury, and Pluto.

Io is the heavenly body with the most active volcanoes. They spit sulfur, giving this satellite an unusual yellow-golden color.

Europa's surface is covered with gigantic frozen "highways." The *Galileo* probe revealed that oceans probably lie under this surface.

The largest natural satellite in the Solar System, **Ganymede**, has a frozen surface covering a rocky core.

Callisto is constantly bombarded by asteroids and comets drawn by Jupiter's gravity.

THE GREAT RED SPOT

The upper portion of the atmosphere is composed of layers of clouds in which violent storms take place. The spectacular Great Red Spot is a huge hurricane that has been raging for more than three centuries; its diameter is more than twice the size of Earth's.

Saturn ♄

The splendid ringed planet

Saturn, with a yellowish tint, is the second-largest planet in the Solar System. Like Jupiter, it is made almost entirely of hydrogen and helium. Its famous rings form a band of about 125,000 miles (200,000 km) in diameter — equivalent to about half the distance from Earth to the Moon — but their maximum thickness is only a few hundred yards (a few hundred m).

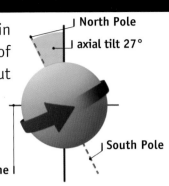

North Pole

axial tilt 27°

South Pole

orbital plane

SATURN'S NATURAL SATELLITES

Saturn has thirty moons that we know of. Some are several thousand miles (several thousand km) in diameter, while others (possibly captured asteroids) are only 12–18 miles (20–30 km) in diameter. Most of Saturn's moons are made of ice mixed with methane, ammonia, and carbon dioxide.

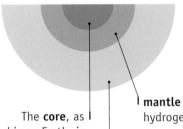

The **core**, as big as Earth, is made of iron and rock.

mantle of metallic hydrogen

As they get farther from the planet's core, the hydrogen and helium layers become more and more liquid and gaseous.

Mimas has a crater called Herschel, which covers one-third of its entire area.

Titan is one-and-a-half times the size of Earth's Moon. It has an atmosphere rich in nitrogen and organic composites, a little like Earth's when it was young.

Dione has craters and perhaps ice deposits.

Rhea is formed of impact craters and rock-hard ice.

Iapetus presents a surface of contrasts: the light part is made of ice, while the dark part is made of an unknown material.

THE SYSTEM OF RINGS

From a distance, Saturn's rings resemble a disk of solid matter. In fact, they are made of many blocks of ice and dust that orbit the planet in a disorganized way. Pictures taken by the *Voyager* probes have revealed thousands of rings with an extraordinarily complex structure. They are divided into seven main sections, from A to G. The Cassini and Encke divisions are the dark areas within the rings.

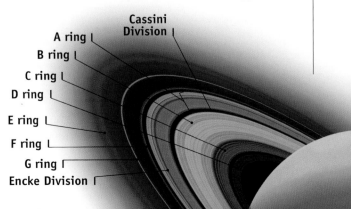

A ring

B ring

C ring

D ring

E ring

F ring

G ring

Encke Division

Cassini Division

Uranus ♅

Uranus was first observed by the astronomer William Herschel, using a telescope, in 1781. The third-largest planet in the Solar System, after Jupiter and Saturn, Uranus is made mainly of rock, ice, and hydrogen.

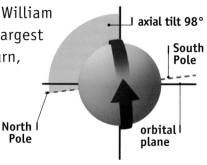

axial tilt 98°

South Pole

North Pole

orbital plane

⌐ Traces of methane in Uranus' **atmosphere** give it a blue-green color.

Curiously, unlike the other planets, Uranus orbits like a top lying on its side.

Eleven **rings** orbit the equator of the planet, which lies on its side. These rings, as dark as Jupiter's, seem to be made of dust and rocks.

Uranus' poles point toward the Sun; each is lit for forty-two years, then plunged into darkness for forty-two years. Uranus takes eighty-four years to revolve around the Sun.

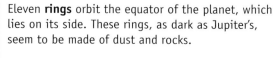

ice

hydrogen and helium

core of rock

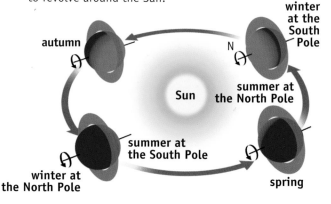

autumn

winter at the South Pole

N

summer at the North Pole

Sun

summer at the South Pole

winter at the North Pole

spring

THE MOONS OF URANUS

Uranus has at least twenty-one satellites: five outer moons, eleven small inner moons, which were discovered by the *Voyager 2* probe in 1986, and five recently discovered moons (since 1997).

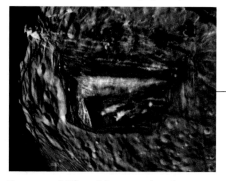

The dark **Umbriel**

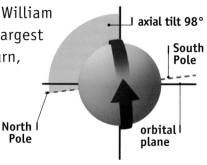

Ariel, Uranus' brightest moon

Oberon, Uranus' most distant satellite.

The largest of Uranus' satellites, **Titania**

Because of **Miranda**'s unusual surface, scientists have theorized that this moon broke apart under the impact of a meteoroid and that the parts were then reunited by the force of gravity.

Neptune ♆

At the edge of the Solar System

A bluish planet that is very similar to Uranus, Neptune is slightly smaller but has more mass. It was discovered by the astronomer Galle in 1846 from calculations made by the mathematicians Adams and Le Verrier.

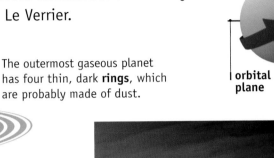

North Pole
axial tilt 30°
South Pole
orbital plane

The outermost gaseous planet has four thin, dark **rings**, which are probably made of dust.

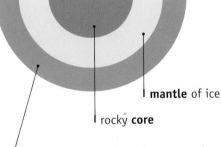

Neptune's **atmosphere** is more active than Uranus'; colored bands, similar to Jupiter's, and small methane clouds have been observed.

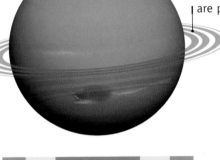

mantle of ice

rocky **core**

Neptune's **atmosphere** is composed of hydrogen, helium, and methane (which gives the planet its blue color).

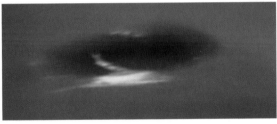

The *Voyager* probe photographed a huge hurricane, similar to Jupiter's Great Red Spot and as big as Earth, called the **Great Dark Spot**. Winds as high as 1,250 miles (2,000 km) per hour, the strongest in the Solar System, have been measured.

NEPTUNE'S NATURAL SATELLITES

Neptune has at least eight natural satellites, including Proteus, 260 miles (420 km) in diameter, Nereid, 220 miles (350 km), and Triton, 1,675 miles (2,700 km). The other five moons, all very dark, are less than 125 miles (200 km) in diameter.

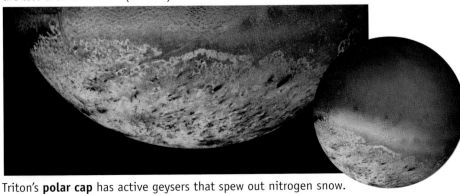

Triton, Neptune's largest satellite, is the coldest object in the Solar System observed by a probe.

Triton's **polar cap** has active geysers that spew out nitrogen snow.

Pluto ♇

Is it really a planet?

Discovered in 1930 by Clyde Tombaugh, Pluto is the only planet that has not been visited by a space probe. It is a very strange object, different from the eight other planets. Because it is about the same size as Earth's Moon, some scientists think of it as an asteroid or a comet.

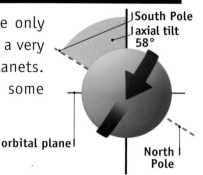

South Pole
axial tilt 58°

orbital plane

North Pole

Pluto may have a thin atmosphere. Its **surface** is probably covered with methane, nitrogen, and carbon dioxide.

Pluto has the most inclined and eccentric **orbit**. It is sometimes closer to the Sun than Neptune is; this was the case between 1979 and 1999.

rock

ice

Pluto is probably 80 percent rocky matter and 20 percent ice, somewhat like Triton (one of Neptune's satellites). Both may actually be objects from the Kuiper Belt of comets at the edge of our Solar System.

Pluto

A DOUBLE PLANET?

Pluto and its satellite, Charon, have a similar size and mass, and these two bodies revolve around each other, always presenting the same side to each other.

Earth

The average **distance** between Pluto and Charon is 12,170 miles (19,600 km).

Charon

Pluto is so small and so far from the Sun that little is known with certainty about it. Recent pictures from the Hubble Space Telescope have given us unprecedented views of Pluto and its satellite, Charon.

The Stars

The Sun, with nine fascinating planets revolving around it, is only one of billions of stars in the Universe. Although we see a bit of the Universe when we look up at the sky, there are in fact hundreds of billions of other stars, large and small, being born and dying, their life and fate governed by their mass.

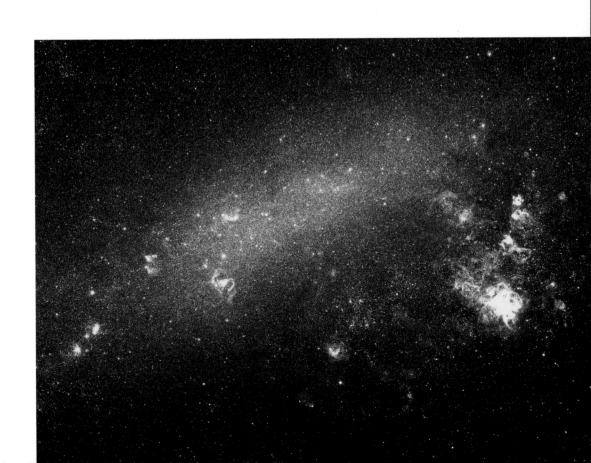

The Stars

Where Do Stars Come from?

Heat in the heart of nebulae

Each year, new stars form within nebulae. They are host to extraordinary nuclear reactions that consume millions of tons of fuel every second. Our own Sun has enough of a hydrogen reserve — some 2 billion trillion tons — that the nuclear reaction sparked 5 billion years ago will continue for just as long into the future.

the Trifid Nebula

THE BIRTH OF STARS

Stars are born within an immense cloud of hydrogen and dust called a nebula.

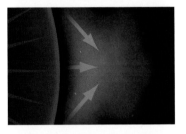

The explosion of one or several nearby stars strikes the nebula, and gravity begins to take effect.

The cloud slowly contracts under the effect of gravity, and material begins to conglomerate naturally.

The cloud begins to rotate, and its temperature climbs. A star embryo (or protostar) forms. Soon, a nuclear reaction begins.

The protostar then becomes a star that will shine until its reserve of hydrogen has been completely converted into helium.

A NUCLEAR REACTION BILLIONS OF YEARS LONG

Pressure in a star's core can create a temperature of 27 million degrees F (15 million degrees C), as in our Sun. Under such conditions, hydrogen nuclei (protons) ❶ stick together to form heavy hydrogen (deuteron) nuclei ❷, which incorporate another proton ❸ to form light helium nuclei ❹. Two light-helium nuclei fuse to create common form of helium ❺. At each stage, energy is released as light (photons) ❻.

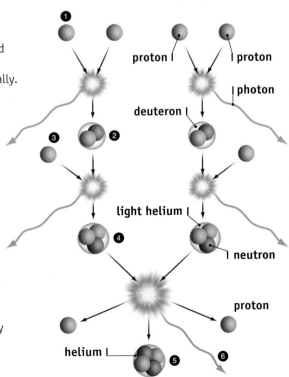

Multiple Stars

We tend to think of stars as solitary objects that form within a cloud of matter (a nebula), becoming a center around which a family of planets develops. This scenario, which occurred for our Solar System, is in fact the exception.

Scientists estimate that at least two-thirds of all stars in our galaxy form systems of two or more stars orbiting around each other, united by their mutual gravitational pull. Unlike our Sun, most stars develop in groups of two or three and sometimes up to seven.

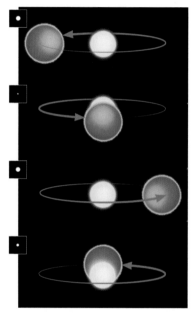

Some stars, known as "false doubles," such as Alcor and Mizar in Ursa Major, can be seen by the naked eye. Others can be seen only with the help of a telescope and sufficient enlargement. False doubles are unrelated stars that happen to lie in the same line of sight.

The star **Algol**, in the constellation Perseus, seems to vary in luminosity. In fact, it is a double star in which the brighter of the pair is periodically occulted by its darker companion, which explains why the brightness of the main star seems to drop at regular intervals.

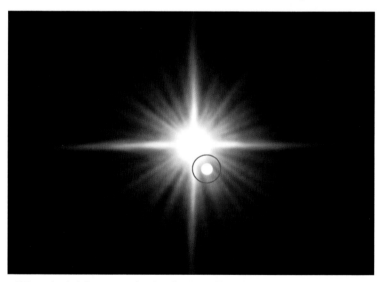

Sirius, the brightest star in the sky, is really a double star. Its companion is a white dwarf called **Sirius B**.

VARIABLE STARS

Variable stars are stars whose brightness varies, either regularly or not. Many of them are pulsating variables that appear to expand and contract. **Mira**, whose size and brightness vary in an eleven-month cycle, is a pulsating variable. During its cycle, it seems to appear, then disappear; it is brightest when it is smallest. Mira also has a small blue companion.

| minimum brightness | brighter | maximum brightness | less bright | minimum brightness |

Classification of Stars

The Hertzsprung-Russell diagram

In the early twentieth century, two astronomers named Hertzsprung and Russell devised a chart that establishes a relationship between a star's luminosity, mass, and temperature. On this chart, the vast majority of stars form a curved diagonal band called the "main sequence." These stars are in their maturity — the period during which they transform their reserves of hydrogen into helium — while those outside the band are being born or dying; 95 percent of observed stars are within the main-sequence band.

At the top of the curved band are the large blue stars, whose temperature is above 45,000° F (25,000° C). In the center are medium-sized white and yellow stars, whose temperature is around 10,800° F (6,000° C), while the small, dim red stars are at the bottom of the band.

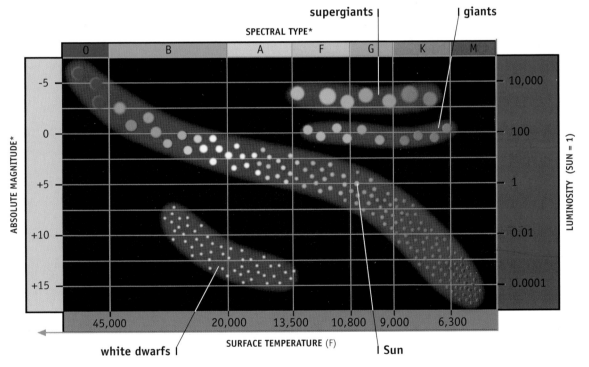

*Absolute magnitude represents the brightness of stars: negative values are accorded to brighter stars. The spectral type designates the color and temperature of a star in relation to its composition.

THE SIZE OF STARS

The supergiant Betelgeuse is one thousand times larger than our Sun, which is a dwarf star. In comparison, white dwarfs are one hundred times smaller than our Sun, and neutron stars are one hundred thousand times smaller.

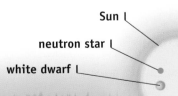

Betelgeuse

Low-mass Stars

The fate of small stars

Even though it seems that they never change, stars in fact undergo a number of transformations. The fate of these objects — their life and their death — is governed by their mass. The Sun, a medium-sized star, will take 10 billion years to transform its hydrogen into helium, and it will end life as a white dwarf. Smaller stars will take tens or even hundreds of billion years to consume their fuel and meet the same fate.

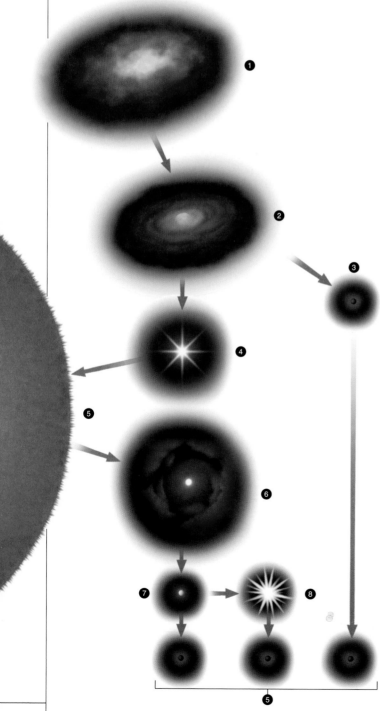

A LONG PROCESS

Stars are born in an immense cloud of hydrogen and dust called a nebula ❶. Little by little, the cloud contracts; the increased pressure causes the temperature to rise. A protostar ❷ forms. It will take tens of millions of years for it to become a star.

If the protostar has insufficient mass to cause a nuclear reaction, it becomes a brown dwarf ❸. A protostar with greater mass triggers a process of thermonuclear fusion and begins its adult life; it becomes a main-sequence star ❹. This is the case for our Sun right now.

After about 10 billion years, the star becomes a red giant ❺ one hundred times the diameter of the Sun, and hundreds of times as bright. Gradually, the outer layers of the red giant dissipate into space. Lit by the core of the star, they form a planetary nebula ❻ for about 1 billion years.

Gradually, the core of the star contracts until it is the size of Earth. The star becomes a white dwarf ❼, an object of enormous density. If the white dwarf has a companion star, it will suck in its material and become an extremely bright nova ❽. The star will eventually grow dimmer until it completely disappears. After a few billion years, it is simply a dead star, a black dwarf ❺.

THE DEATH OF A STAR

At the end of their lives, small stars become **white dwarfs**, the remains of a once bright star, but now very dense.

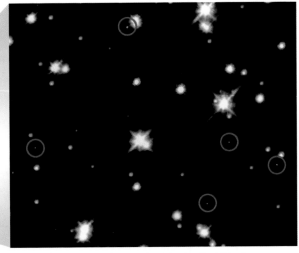

The M4 star cluster, observed from Earth.

The same cluster observed with the Hubble Space Telescope. The white dwarfs are circled. They represent about 10 percent of all stars.

A SPECTACULAR PHENOMENON

A white dwarf that suddenly transforms itself into a very bright star is called a nova, which means "new star." Every year, about fifty stars in the Milky Way become novas.

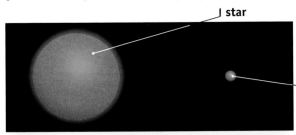

star

white dwarf

The process that gives birth to a nova is likely to occur when a white dwarf is close to another star.

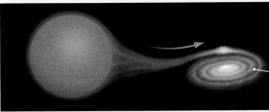

accretion disk

The white dwarf sometimes sucks up part of its companion's material. This material accumulates on its surface and forms an accretion disk.

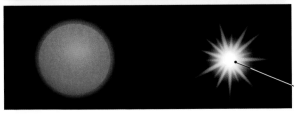

nova

The temperature rises, causing a huge explosion. A nova then appears bright in the sky. In one year, this "new star" emits more energy than does the Sun in a million years.

A FAILED STAR

Brown dwarfs are larger than planets, but their mass is too low to trigger a nuclear reaction. In the photograph: a tiny brown dwarf beside the star Gliese 229.

The Stars

Massive Stars

A brilliant fate

Massive stars evolve differently from small stars. The life of a massive star is shorter but more spectacular: in each stage of its life it is brighter than a small star, and it goes from one stage to the next more quickly because it burns its fuel more rapidly. While small stars take billions of years to transform their hydrogen into helium, massive stars do so in several million years and then become supernovæ.

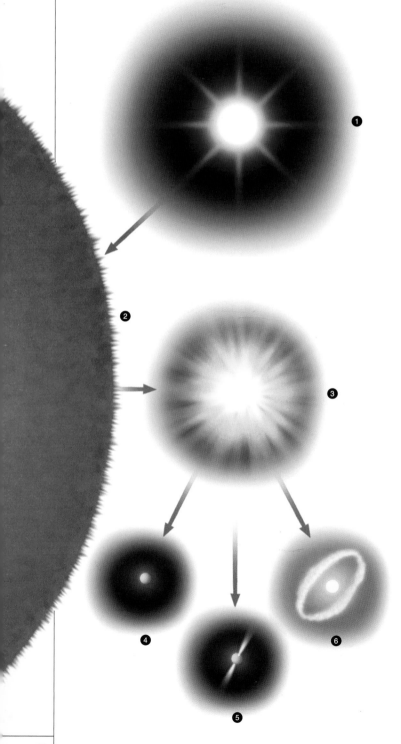

EXTREME ENERGY AND DENSITY

Massive stars develop similarly to small stars, becoming main-sequence stars ❶.

After 500 million years, the star becomes a supergiant ❷ with a diameter five hundred times the Sun's and ten thousand times its luminosity. Unlike a small star, a massive star then continues the fusion process, producing the first twenty-six chemical elements, up to iron.

In less than one second, the star collapses in on itself and explodes with such intensity that it liberates more energy than billions of suns; it is now a supernova ❸. For several weeks, it burns more brightly than the billions of stars that make up its galaxy.

The supernova leaves behind it a remnant core of collapsed matter: a neutron star ❹, which contains as much matter as the Sun concentrated in a space the size of a large city. It is an incredibly dense object. A neutron star that rotates rapidly is a pulsar ❺. If the remains of the supernova are more than three times the mass of the Sun, the matter continues to condense until it becomes a black hole ❻.

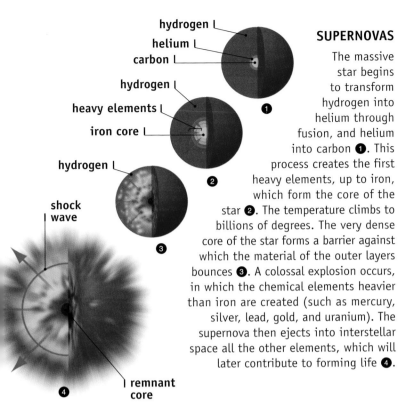

hydrogen
helium
carbon

➊

hydrogen
heavy elements
iron core

➋

hydrogen

➌

shock wave

remnant core

➍

SUPERNOVAS

The massive star begins to transform hydrogen into helium through fusion, and helium into carbon ➊. This process creates the first heavy elements, up to iron, which form the core of the star ➋. The temperature climbs to billions of degrees. The very dense core of the star forms a barrier against which the material of the outer layers bounces ➌. A colossal explosion occurs, in which the chemical elements heavier than iron are created (such as mercury, silver, lead, gold, and uranium). The supernova then ejects into interstellar space all the other elements, which will later contribute to forming life ➍.

In February 1987 a supergiant in the Large Magellanic Cloud exploded and became **Supernova 1987a** (above), the closest and brightest supernova observed in almost four centuries. Top: a photograph taken shortly before the star exploded.

NEUTRON STARS AND PULSARS

As its name indicates, the neutron star is made mainly of extremely compressed neutrons, resulting from the combination of electrons and protons that fused when the supernova exploded. A pulsar (a contraction of "pulsating star") is a neutron star that rotates very rapidly, emitting a regular radio signal. The two poles of the star's intense magnetic field each produce an electromagnetic beam.

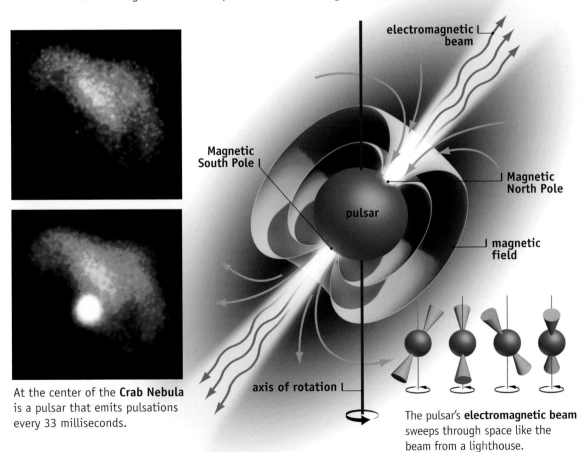

electromagnetic beam

Magnetic South Pole

Magnetic North Pole

pulsar

magnetic field

axis of rotation

At the center of the **Crab Nebula** is a pulsar that emits pulsations every 33 milliseconds.

The pulsar's **electromagnetic beam** sweeps through space like the beam from a lighthouse.

Strange Black Holes

The ultimate fate of massive stars

Some stars, ones that are tens of times more massive than the Sun, have an unusual fate. Their core collapses on itself until it completely disappears and becomes a black hole — the final stage in the star's life. The gravitational force of a black hole is so intense that nothing can escape it, not even light!

It is such a strange phenomenon that it cannot be seen in and of itself. On the other hand, we can observe the effects that it has on the space around it.

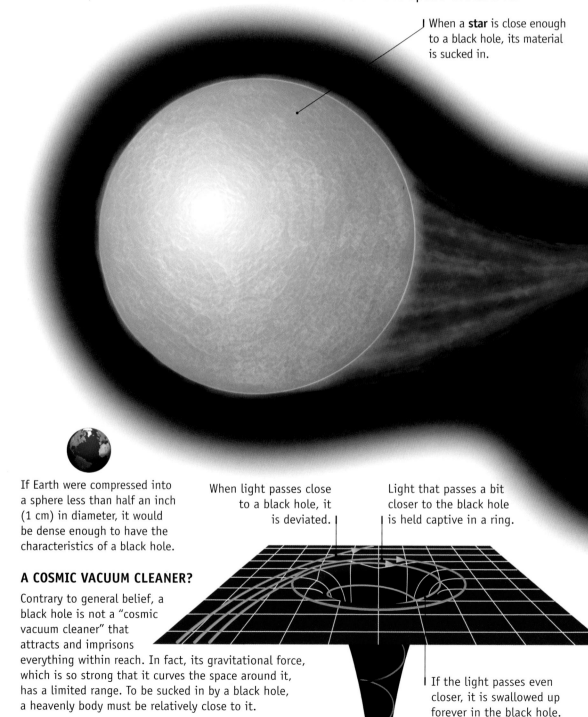

When a **star** is close enough to a black hole, its material is sucked in.

If Earth were compressed into a sphere less than half an inch (1 cm) in diameter, it would be dense enough to have the characteristics of a black hole.

When light passes close to a black hole, it is deviated.

Light that passes a bit closer to the black hole is held captive in a ring.

A COSMIC VACUUM CLEANER?

Contrary to general belief, a black hole is not a "cosmic vacuum cleaner" that attracts and imprisons everything within reach. In fact, its gravitational force, which is so strong that it curves the space around it, has a limited range. To be sucked in by a black hole, a heavenly body must be relatively close to it.

If the light passes even closer, it is swallowed up forever in the black hole.

HOW DOES A BLACK HOLE FORM?

After a massive star explodes (supernova), what remains of its core begins to contract, exerting an extraordinarily strong gravitational force. At the surface of the star, light is still able to escape ❶. Little by little, the rays are curved under the effect of constantly growing gravity ❷ until they can no longer escape ❸. The star finally collapses on itself, becoming a zero-volume of infinitely dense matter; this is a black hole ❹ from which nothing, not even photons of light, escapes. It is therefore invisible.

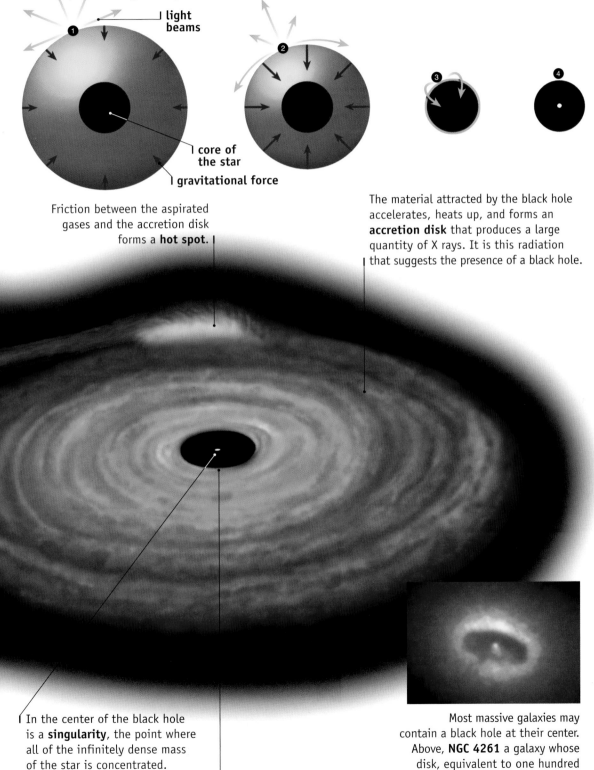

light beams

core of the star

gravitational force

Friction between the aspirated gases and the accretion disk forms a **hot spot.**

The material attracted by the black hole accelerates, heats up, and forms an **accretion disk** that produces a large quantity of X rays. It is this radiation that suggests the presence of a black hole.

In the center of the black hole is a **singularity**, the point where all of the infinitely dense mass of the star is concentrated.

The **event horizon** marks the limit beyond which material is imprisoned.

Most massive galaxies may contain a black hole at their center. Above, **NGC 4261** a galaxy whose disk, equivalent to one hundred thousand suns, is attracted to a black hole at the center.

Star Clusters

Vast concentrations of stars

Stars are born by the dozen within star nurseries, clouds containing a multitude of stars. The phenomenon sometimes gives rise to enchantingly beautiful star clusters.

In these clusters we can observe, all at once in a relatively small area, the evolution of various types of stars (from small red stars to solar types to blue giants) at the same time.

OPEN CLUSTERS

An open cluster, also called a galactic cluster, is a small, irregularly shaped group of stars. It contains from several hundred to several thousand stars and occupies a relatively small area. It is in fact a star nursery — a place where we can observe stars just a few million years old. Large blue stars, which have a short life, are found in this kind of cluster. Since open clusters also contain much gas and dust, they provide beautiful cosmic landscapes.

The **Pleiades** open cluster, located in the Northern Hemisphere, is made up of several thousand stars. It contains the Seven Sisters, which are visible to the naked eye.

A detail of a spectacular photograph taken by the Hubble Space Telescope shows the process of star formation in the **Eagle Nebula**. The peaks of gas at the top of the column surround new stars.

It is estimated that there are about fifteen hundred open clusters in the Milky Way. All of these clusters are located within our galaxy's disk.

GLOBULAR CLUSTERS

A globular cluster is a spherical cloud that generally contains hundreds of thousands or millions of stars. Unlike an open cluster, a globular cluster contains older stars and therefore few blue giants. This type of cluster is also almost devoid of gas or interstellar dust. The concentration of stars in a globular cluster is dozens of times as high as in an open cluster.

With two or three million stars, 47 Toucana is a well-known globular cluster in the Southern Hemisphere. Its luminosity is half a million times greater than that of our Sun.

Some 150 globular clusters have been observed throughout our galaxy, forming a spherical halo. These clusters were formed even before the Milky Way.

Constellations

Orienting ourselves in the sky

If we view the sky far from all ambient light, we can see up to three thousand stars in each hemisphere. To guide themselves among this myriad of stars, our ancient ancestors created constellations, which enabled them to divide the thousands of stars visible to the naked eye into groups that they could memorize.

Over time, we have populated the sky with a growing number of figures of all sorts, including geometric shapes and representations of animals and mythological characters, many of which are attached to a story or legend. In 1929, the International Astronomical Union defined the regions of the sky enclosing the eighty-eight constellations we recognize today.

THE ZODIAC

Earth's annual trajectory passes twelve of these constellations. This path through the heavens is called the Zodiac, and the Moon, the Sun, and the planets seem to move along it. The constellations are never more than 40° from the celestial equator. Depending on the time of year, different constellations are visible at night from Earth. In March, for instance, we see the constellations of Leo and Virgo.

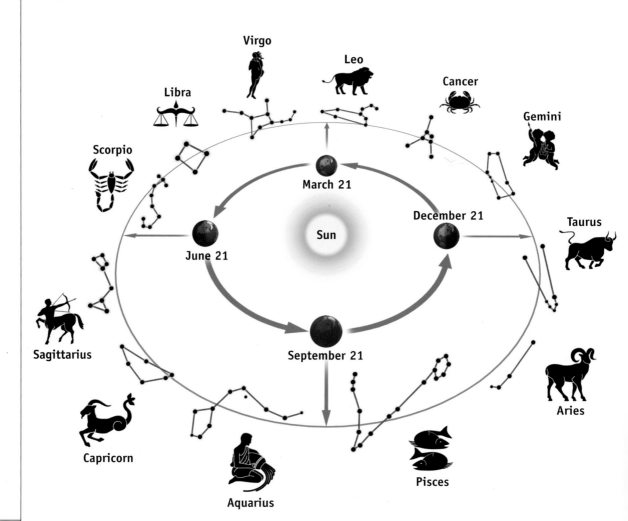

DECEIVING APPEARANCES

Constellations are arbitrary groupings of stars. Most of the time, the stars in a constellation are very distant from one another, and the apparent shape that they trace in the sky results from an effect of perspective. This is the case for the eight stars that make up the Big Dipper: the two farthest stars, Alkaid and Dubhe, are dozens of light-years (LY) from the other stars in the constellation.

A light-year (LY) is the distance light travels in a vacuum in one year.
1 LY = about 5.878 trillion miles
(9.46 trillion km)

Alkaid

Alcor

Mizar

Alioth

Megrez

Phekda

Dubhe

Merak

Earth

50 LY

70 LY   90 LY   110 LY   130 LY

FROM ONE HEMISPHERE TO THE OTHER

In the sky are about six thousand stars visible to the naked eye, grouped into eighty-eight constellations. It is impossible to see all of the constellations from any one spot on the globe; on the other hand, some of the constellations from each hemisphere can be seen from the equator. This is why some constellations in the Southern Hemisphere can also be seen in the Northern Hemisphere, and vice versa.

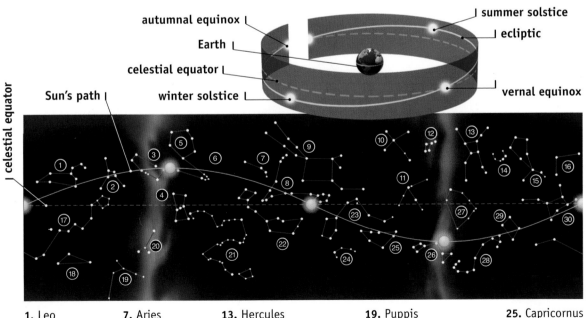

autumnal equinox

Earth

celestial equator

Sun's path   winter solstice

summer solstice

ecliptic

vernal equinox

celestial equator

1. Leo	7. Aries	13. Hercules	19. Puppis	25. Capricornus
2. Cancer	8. Pisces	14. Corona Borealis	20. Canis Major	26. Sagittarius
3. Gemini	9. Pegasus	15. Bootes	21. Eridanus	27. Ophiuchus
4. Orion	10. Cygnus	16. Coma Berenices	22. Cetus	28. Scorpius
5. Auriga	11. Aquila	17. Hydra	23. Aquarius	29. Libra
6. Taurus	12. Lyra	18. Antlia	24. Pisces Austrinus	30. Virgo

The Constellations of the Northern Hemisphere

A stroll through the skies

The northern sky looks away from the center of our galaxy. The constellations of this hemisphere are not visible from far southern latitudes. On the other hand, in northern Europe and North America some constellations, including Ursa Major ❸❷ and Ursa Minor ❷❶, can be seen every night of the year.

Other constellations are relatively easy to locate, among them the huge square of Pegasus, formed by four bright stars. The constellation Cygnus ⓫ contains Deneb, a star 70,000 times as bright as the Sun.

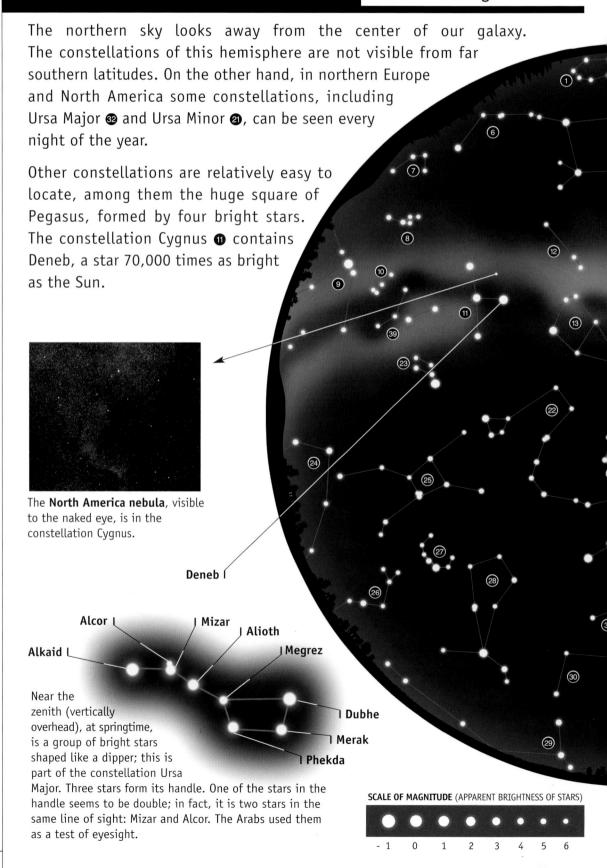

The **North America nebula**, visible to the naked eye, is in the constellation Cygnus.

Deneb

Alcor | Mizar | Alioth | Megrez

Alkaid |

Near the zenith (vertically overhead), at springtime, is a group of bright stars shaped like a dipper; this is part of the constellation Ursa Major. Three stars form its handle. One of the stars in the handle seems to be double; in fact, it is two stars in the same line of sight: Mizar and Alcor. The Arabs used them as a test of eyesight.

| Dubhe

| Merak

| Phekda

SCALE OF MAGNITUDE (APPARENT BRIGHTNESS OF STARS)

- 1   0   1   2   3   4   5   6

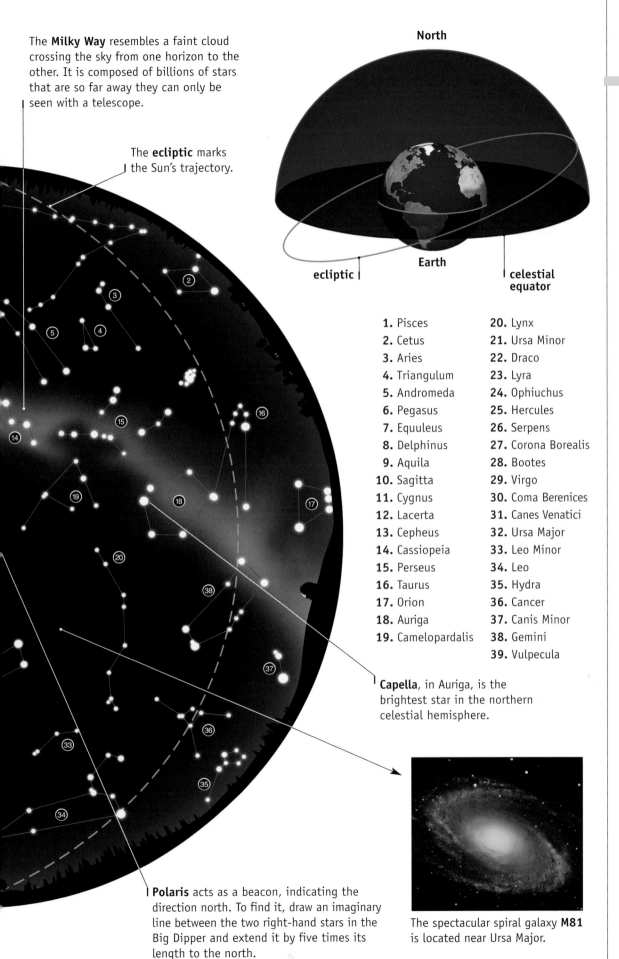

The **Milky Way** resembles a faint cloud crossing the sky from one horizon to the other. It is composed of billions of stars that are so far away they can only be seen with a telescope.

The **ecliptic** marks the Sun's trajectory.

North

Earth

ecliptic

celestial equator

1. Pisces
2. Cetus
3. Aries
4. Triangulum
5. Andromeda
6. Pegasus
7. Equuleus
8. Delphinus
9. Aquila
10. Sagitta
11. Cygnus
12. Lacerta
13. Cepheus
14. Cassiopeia
15. Perseus
16. Taurus
17. Orion
18. Auriga
19. Camelopardalis

20. Lynx
21. Ursa Minor
22. Draco
23. Lyra
24. Ophiuchus
25. Hercules
26. Serpens
27. Corona Borealis
28. Bootes
29. Virgo
30. Coma Berenices
31. Canes Venatici
32. Ursa Major
33. Leo Minor
34. Leo
35. Hydra
36. Cancer
37. Canis Minor
38. Gemini
39. Vulpecula

Capella, in Auriga, is the brightest star in the northern celestial hemisphere.

Polaris acts as a beacon, indicating the direction north. To find it, draw an imaginary line between the two right-hand stars in the Big Dipper and extend it by five times its length to the north.

The spectacular spiral galaxy **M81** is located near Ursa Major.

Glossary

accretion: The process by which material agglomerates under the effect of gravity to form massive celestial bodies such as stars, planets, and galaxies.

accretion disk: Flat rotating disk of matter that orbits a star, a black hole, or any other massive body.

aphelion: For an object that orbits the Sun, the point on its orbit that is farthest from the Sun.

convection: In a gas or liquid, the transfer of heat through movement.

deuteron: Nucleus of a deuterium atom, a stable isotope of hydrogen (also called heavy hydrogen), consisting of one proton and one neutron.

ecliptic: The plane of Earth's orbit relative to the Sun; also, the Sun's apparent path among the stars.

helium: Chemical element whose nucleus is formed of two protons and two neutrons, around which two electrons orbit. It is a very light gas found in great quantities in stars (including the Sun).

hydrogen: The lightest and most abundant known chemical element in the Universe. The nucleus of hydrogen is composed of one proton, around which one electron orbits.

inclination: Angle between an object's celestial equator and its orbital plane, or the angle between an object's axis of rotation and the perpendicular of the orbital plane.

infrared waves: Electromagnetic radiation whose wavelength is slightly longer than that of visible light: heat.

ion: An atom that has lost or gained one or more electrons.

isotope: An atom that has the same number of protons as a particular chemical element but a different number of neutrons. For example, a hydrogen nucleus contains one proton and no neutrons; one hydrogen isotope, deuterium (heavy hydrogen), contains one proton and one neutron.

light-year: Distance traveled by light at the speed of about 5.878 trillion miles (9.46 trillion km) per year.

magnetic field: The region surrounding an object within which a magnetic force is exerted on electrically charged particles.

main sequence: A major grouping of stars, one that contains the Sun and about 95 percent of observed stars; these stars are in their maturity — the period during which they transform their reserves of hydrogen into helium; stars that are outside the main sequence are being born or are dying.

nebula: Cloud of gas and dust in which stars are born.

NGC: Abbreviation for *New General Catalogue of Nebulae and Star Clusters*. This document is used to identify celestial objects that are not stars.

nuclear fusion: Nuclear reaction in which atomic nuclei combine to form larger nuclei, releasing an enormous amount of energy.

orbit: The path of a celestial object as it revolves around a planet or star.

perihelion: For an object orbiting the Sun, the point in its orbit that is closest to the Sun.

photon: Particle that transmits electromagnetic radiation, including visible light.

proto-: Prefix used in astronomy to designate a celestial object that is being formed (for example, protoplanet, protostar, or protogalaxy).

proton: Particle with a positive charge; component of the atomic nucleus.

thermonuclear reaction: Nuclear reaction that takes place in the heart of a star, during which hydrogen nuclei fuse into helium, emitting a large amount of energy in the form of light and heat.

Universe: Everything that exists as a whole, including all objects in space.

zenith: The point in the sky situated directly over an observer's head.

zodiac: The band of twelve constellations circling the celestial sphere and crossing the Sun's trajectory (Aries, Taurus, Gemini, Cancer, Leo, Virgo, Libra, Scorpio, Sagittarius, Capricorn, Aquarius, Pisces).

Books

Asteroids: A History. Curtis Peebles (Dover Publications)

Burnham's Celestial Handbook. Robert Burnham and Herbert A. Luft (Dover Publications)

A Field Guide to the Stars and Planets. Jay M. Pasachoff (Houghton Mifflin Co.)

The Hatfield Photographic Lunar Atlas. Jeremy Cook (Springer Verlag)

The New Solar System. J. Kelly Beatty et al, editors (Cambridge University Press)

Other Worlds: Images of the Cosmos from Earth and Space. James S. Trefil (National Geographic Society)

The Planet Observer's Handbook. Fred William Price and John E. Westfall (Cambridge University Press)

Sky Atlas 2000.0 Deluxe. Wil Tirion and Roger W. Sinnott (Cambridge University Press)

Star-Hopping: Your Visa to Viewing the Universe. Robert A. Garfinkle (Cambridge University Press)

Stars (Scientific American Library No. 39). James B. Kaler (W. H. Freeman and Co.)

The Stars: A New Way to See Them. Hans Augusto Rey (Houghton Mifflin Co.)

Videos

2001: A Space Odyssey. (Turner Home Entertainment)

Dune. (MCA Home Video)

Mars: The Red Planet. (D3/Digital Disc)

Mission to Mars. (Video)

Nova: Runaway Universe. (WGBH)

Standard Deviants: Astronomy, Part I. (Cerebellum Corp.)

Stephen Hawking's Universe. (PBS Home Video)

The Voyager Odyssey. (Image Entertainment)

Web Sites

The Astronomy Page
www.theschoolpage.com/astro.htm

The Nine Planets: A Multimedia Tour of the Solar System
www.nineplanets.org/

Solar System Exploration
sse.jpl.nasa.gov/

Welcome to the Planets, Cal Tech
pds.jpl.nasa.gov/planets/

Index